FASHION UPCYCLING

The DIY Guide to Sewing, Mending, and Sustainably Reinventing Your Wardrobe

YSABEL HILADO

Fashion Upcycling:

The DIY Guide to Sewing, Mending, and Sustainably Reinventing Your Wardrobe

Ysabel Hilado

www.ysabelhilado.com
Social media @ysabelhilado

Editor: Kelly Reed
Project manager: Lisa Brazieal
Marketing coordinator: Katie Walker
Copyeditor: Linda Laflamme
Proofreader: Patricia Pane
Interior design: Aren Straiger
Interior layout: Danielle Foster
Cover production: Aren Straiger
Cover photograph: Ashley Chang

ISBN: 979-8-88814-033-8
1st Edition (1st printing, August 2023)
© 2023 Ysabel Hilado
All photographs © Ashley Chang unless otherwise noted.

Rocky Nook Inc.
1010 B Street, Suite 350
San Rafael, CA 94901
USA

www.rockynook.com

Distributed in the UK and Europe by Publishers Group UK
Distributed in the U.S. and all other territories by Ingram Publisher Services

Library of Congress Control Number: 2023938231

This book is printed on acid-free paper.
Printed in China.

TABLE OF CONTENTS

1 THE UPCYCLING PROJECTS

PHOTO BY MIKAEL-ANGELO TE

INTRODUCTION

When I was 13, I came across a picture of an "elephant sweater" on a blogging website called Tumblr. It was a two-tone sweater that had the silhouette of an elephant with its tusk as one arm. I thought it was the coolest sweater I'd ever seen. I couldn't afford the one I saw online, so I decided to try to make it myself. I bought two sweatshirts for under $10 and found my Lola's hand-sewing kit in a cookie tin. I pulled up a picture of the elephant sweater, threaded a needle, and sat on the hardwood floor of my living room. One day later, I had completed my very first sewing and upcycling project ever.

I'm Ysabel Hilado, a fashion designer, upcycler, and digital content creator from Southern California. For over a decade, I've been avidly documenting my fashion journey online. Prior to college, I taught myself how to sew solely through books and online tutorials from Pinterest and YouTube, because in-person sewing classes were too expensive or far from home. I wanted to learn how to sew for two reasons:

1. To recreate the clothing that I saw online and couldn't afford at the mall
2. To start a side hustle so I could make money to hang out with my friends after school

One of my early fashion ventures was Along the Lines Pocket Tees; I sold customized pocket tees out of my locker and shipped orders worldwide for a year. I stopped because I decided to learn the actual process of clothing construction and design instead. Using clothes from a local thrift store, I began to make alterations to my finds to match my personal style. From then on, for any big event in my life—from birthdays to proms to graduation—I attempted to make my own outfit to commemorate the day, then shared the entire process on my blog. I still wasn't sure if I wanted to pursue fashion design as a career, but I slowly started to build a portfolio and even auditioned for *Project Runway: Junior*. I made it all the way through to become one of the 12 teenage fashion designers featured in the show's first season. After that experience, I realized that I was meant to be a designer.

During my six-year college experience, I took any opportunity to build a name for myself outside of my classes and retail jobs. I created collections and took design commissions to practice my skills. Whenever I received a chance to participate in local fashion shows and exhibitions, I used the opportunity to showcase my craft and make connections. For a creative outlet and to help me become better known in the fashion community, I always set aside time to make DIY and design content for social media. In of May 2022, I graduated with my bachelor's degree in fashion design and minor in fashion merchandising from California State University, Long Beach.

By sharing my fashion journey, I hope to inspire others to pursue what they're passionate about in life. To give back to my younger self, I want to work toward making fashion education accessible and attainable. This book is one of many ways to do that, and I hope you enjoy every moment of it.

Hilado

HOW TO GET THE MOST OUT OF THIS BOOK

In this project-based book, you'll find 25 fashionable upcycling tutorials that show you how to transform everyday items, such as shirts, pants, and even blankets, into customized tops, bottoms, and accessories. Have leftover fabric from projects? I'll share some ideas for what you can turn that into, too. The projects cater to a variety of skill levels, and none are restricted to certain measurements, designs, or patterns. You won't need patterns for most of the projects, but for the few that do, I'll show you easy ways to create them. Whether you're just learning how to sew your first stitch or you've been sewing for a decade and want fresh ideas, my hope is that you'll feel inspired through each page and photo. When it comes to upcycling, I encourage you to *have fun*. Don't be afraid to *experiment*.

All the projects can be *customized*. Look at each featured garment as a starting point and build your design from there. It's up to *you* to decide the materials and fabrics you want to work with, the color scheme that speaks to you the most, how short you want a hem, or how wide you want a specific measurement to be. Do not restrict yourself to what you see on the pages! Fashion has *no* limitations; express yourself and showcase your creativity.

WHY UPCYCLE CLOTHES?

Now is a great time for a deep closet cleanout and to *candidly* reflect on each piece you've collected. How often do you wear that sparkly sequined mini-dress at the back of your clothing rack? How about that faded black t-shirt with a cracked screen-printed picture of your favorite band? Was it really five holidays ago when you last wore that cable knit sweater, and where did those holes come from? How about those neon checkered jeans from—ahem—*middle school*? We all have a few pieces in our closets collecting dust, but before you donate them or pass them down, consider giving those garments a second chance at life.

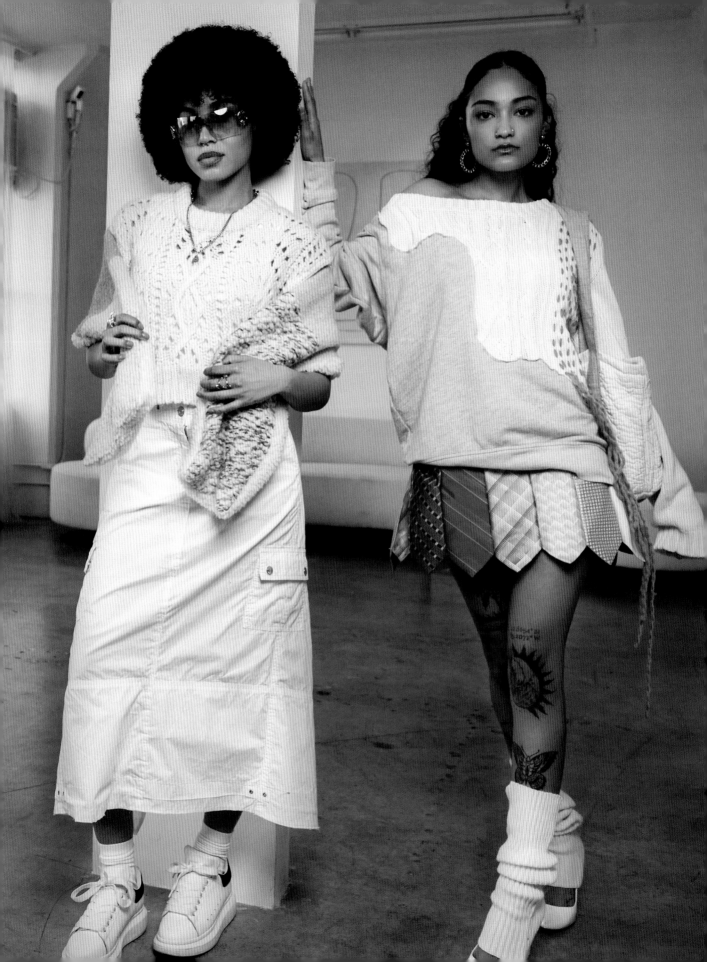

The fashion industry is one the biggest polluting industries in the world. Fast fashion and over-consumption are a large part of the issue. According to Goodonyou.eco, *fast fashion* is defined as "cheap, trendy clothing that samples ideas from the catwalk or celebrity culture and turns them into garments in high-street stores at breakneck speed to meet consumer demand." If you go to a thrift store or secondhand shop, chances are you'll quickly spot one of these fast fashion brands within the first few seconds of searching through the racks.

With the trend cycle moving at an all-time high, big corporations want to keep up with their consumers, resulting in an excessive amount of clothes being made, bought, and discarded. Quality is an insignificant factor as long as the clothing is selling. Many clothing factories are notorious for having unsafe working conditions for underpaid and overworked garment workers. Our environment also suffers from this excess, becoming polluted with microfibers, toxic dyes, and non-biodegradable textiles in landfills.

By upcycling unworn clothing and textiles, you'll repurpose them into one-of-a-kind designs while also saving them from being dumped in a landfill. Look at upcycling as a fun way to tap into your creativity, practice your sewing skills, and get more wear out of the clothes you already have.

WANT MORE INFORMATION?

The True Cost is a documentary film that provides an eye-opening inside look at the social, environmental, and economic impact of fast fashion throughout the world.

The Council of Fashion Designers of America (CFDA) maintains an online Sustainability Resource Hub dedicated to providing educational tools and materials. It features an extensive A–Z directory that highlights various topics, organizations, and foundations working toward a sustainable industry ahead.

Fashion Revolution provides online and printable resources on how global citizens, industry professionals, and educators can get involved and take action in their local communities to support a better future for fashion.

SUPPLY CHECKLIST AND TOOL MUST-HAVES

With all the sewing supplies and tools to choose from, figuring out what you really need can be overwhelming for beginning upcyclers. If you're brand new to building your sewing kit, here are a few starter items you'll want to have on hand:

1. See-through grid ruler
   (This is great for double-checking your measurements before making.)

2. Sewing gauge
   (Use this for quick and precise measurements.)

3. Measuring tape
   (Use this for body measurements.)

4. Tailor's chalk

5. Pins

6. Sewing clips
   (These are great for working with thick fabrics such as denim or leather.)

7. Paper scissors

8. Fabric snips
   (Use these for loose or hanging threads.)

9. Fabric shears
   (Invest in a nice pair to cut smoothly through all your materials and avoid using them on paper to maintain sharpness.)

22

10. Water-soluble marker
    (*Use this to make visible markings on your fabric and remove with water.*)

11. Pen

12. Pencil

13. Eraser

14. Safety pins
    (*Besides holding clothing in place, use these for threading drawstrings through sewn channels.*)

15. Thimble

16. Needle threader
    (*This will aid in guiding your thread through small needle eyes.*)

17. Hand-sewing needles

18. Extra bobbins

19. Seam rippers
    (*Undo mistakes in your sewing with these.*)

20. Thread

21. Sewing machine needles
    (*Keep a variety of sizes ready to match the fabric you're working with.*)

22. Toolbox or large pouch to carry all your tools

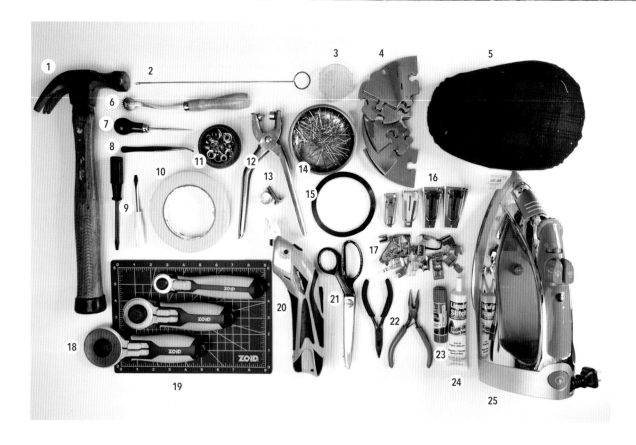

If you want to have a more extensive kit to be prepared for all different types of projects, you can also add these tools and supplies:

1. Hammer
2. Loop turner
3. Beeswax
4. Pattern weights
5. Sewing ham
6. Tracing wheel
7. Awl
8. Tweezers
9. Screwdrivers
10. Scotch tape
11. Eyelets
12. Eyelet press
13. Eyelet tool kit
14. Magnetic bowl
15. Draping tape
16. Bias tape maker
17. A variety of sewing machine foots
18. Rotary cutters
19. Cutting mat
20. Electric scissors
21. Pinking shears
22. Pliers
23. Liquid Stitch glue
24. Glue stick
25. Iron

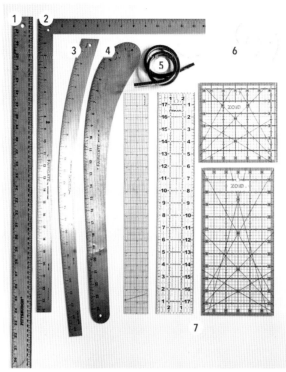

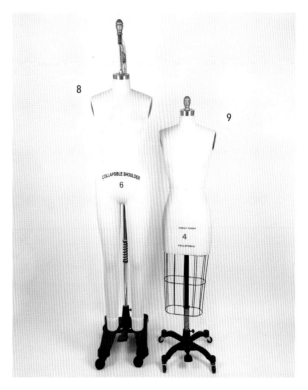

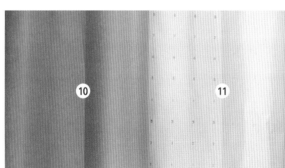

1. Yard stick
2. L-shaped ruler
3. Hip curve
4. Vary form curve
5. Flexible tape
6. French curve ruler
7. Acrylic grid quilting rulers in various sizes
8. Full dress form
9. Half dress form
10. Kraft paper
11. Pattern paper

WHERE TO BUY TOOLS AND SUPPLIES

To purchase supplies, check out your local craft or fabric store. For online shopping, Wawak.com is a great resource for all your sewing needs. Don't forget to check for online coupons!

Secondhand shopping sites such as OfferUp.com and Facebook Marketplace may also have supplies in your area.

SEWING BASICS TO KNOW

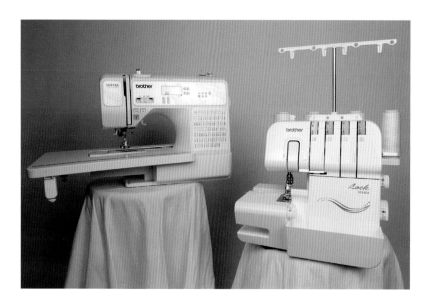

If you've never touched a sewing machine or needle in your life, don't be afraid! This book is meant to help you practice your skills as you move along in your sewing and upcycling journey. Here's a rundown of some sewing basics that'll help you navigate each upcycling project with ease.

PICK YOUR SEWING METHOD

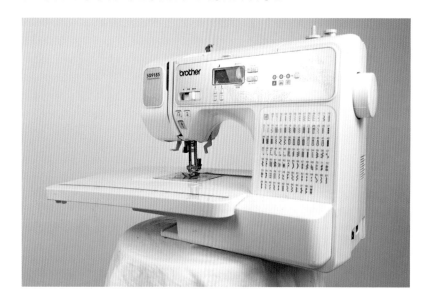

Sewing machine

You do not need to have the latest and greatest machine to complete a sewing project. A regular home machine with a few simple stitches will allow you to create beautiful pieces. If your machine can do a straight stitch, back stitch, and zigzag stitch, you're good to go! Keep in mind that no two machines are the same and some features vary, so play around with your stitches to get acquainted.

Needle and thread

Hand sewing is the most common way many people get introduced to sewing. All you need is a pack of needles and thread. Needles come in a variety of sizes, and you'll get the best results when you pick a needle that matches your fabric. If you're working with a thick fabric, such as denim, opt for a thicker needle. If you're working with silk chiffon,

pick a thinner needle so it doesn't pull any threads. Beyond your needle and thread, a few add-ons will come in handy too.

WHAT ABOUT A SERGER/OVERLOCK OR COVERSTITCH MACHINE?

A *serger* cleans up raw edges on your fabric. If you're new to the world of sewing, a serger isn't necessary. Once you build more confidence in your skills, however, it is definitely a great investment!

A *coverstitch* machine creates clean hems on many knit, jersey, and stretch fabrics. Unless you plan on working with a lot of those fabrics in the future, you won't typically need a coverstitch machine when you're starting your sewing journey.

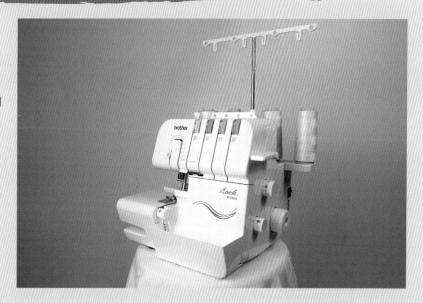

A *thimble* is great to prevent you from poking your finger and can help when pushing your needle through thick, stubborn fabrics.

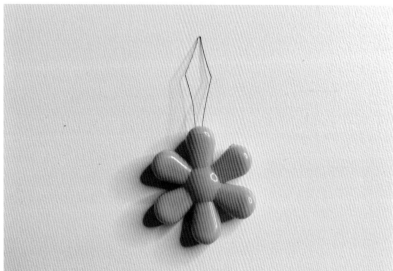

A *needle threader* can help you pull your thread through the eye—especially with fine needles.

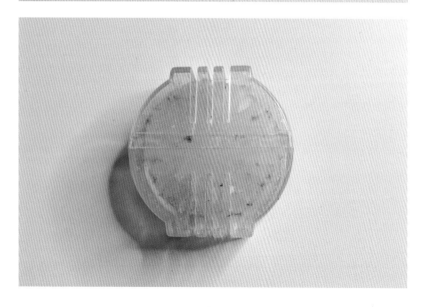

Coating your thread with *beeswax* reduces tangles and knots while sewing.

PRACTICE SEWING SAMPLES

Creating a variety of samples is a great way to get used to your machine and practice a new skill. *Muslin*, a woven cotton fabric, is a general choice for creating any type of sample before cutting into your main fabric. If you don't have muslin, choose a practice fabric that closely resembles the material you plan to use for your project.

With your needle or sewing machine ready, grab your practice fabric and try the following basic techniques. You'll use them throughout the book's sewing projects, so investing the time now will make things go more smoothly later.

HOW TO SEW A STRAIGHT LINE

Needle-and-thread method

A *running stitch* is the simplest way to sew a straight line. Basically, you weave the thread in and out of your fabric at equal lengths.

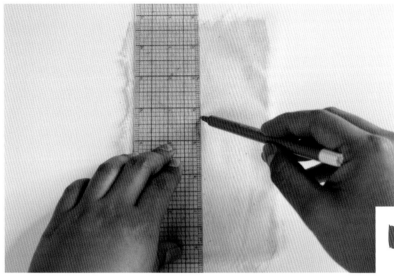

STEP 1

On a cut piece of fabric, draw a straight line in the middle using a ruler and marking tool of your choice.

STEP 2

Choose a needle and some thread that contrasts with the fabric.

Thread your needle. Double your thread to lessen the chance of breakage.

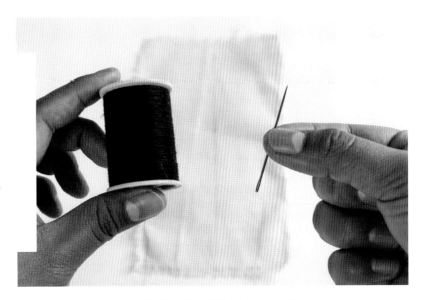

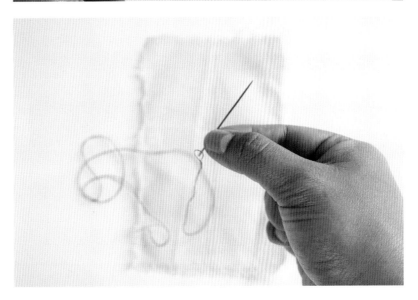

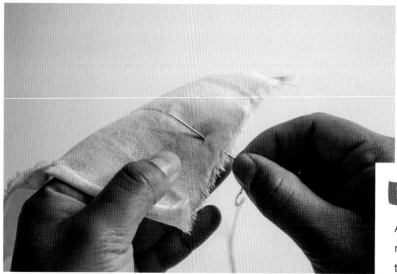

STEP 3

At the start of your line, you need a knot to secure your thread. To create one, first pull your needle up through the fabric from the wrong side.

Leave a small amount of thread on the wrong side of the fabric.

STEP 4

With your needle, scoop up a small section of fabric.

STEP 5

Create a loop.

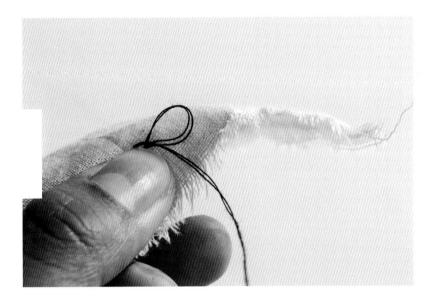

STEP 6

Pull your thread through the loop to secure it.

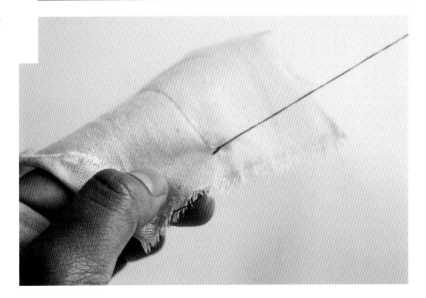

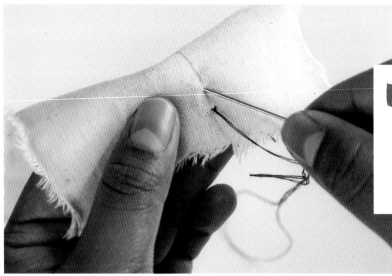

STEP 7

Begin your running stitch by putting your needle down through the front side of fabric and back up.

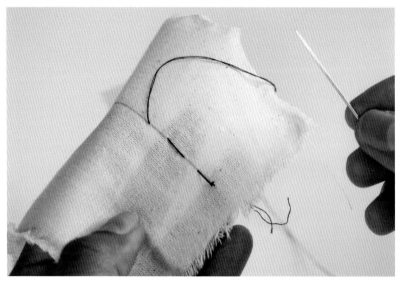

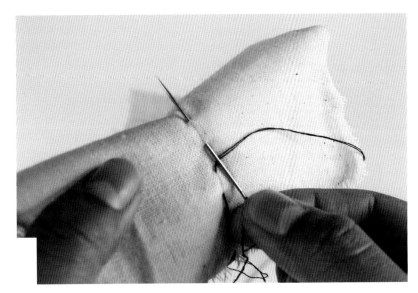

STEP 8

Pull your stitch through and repeat.

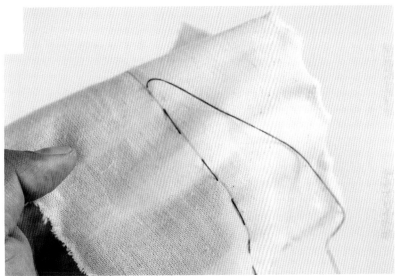

STEP 9

You can do multiple stitches at a time by bunching your fabric and pulling your thread through.

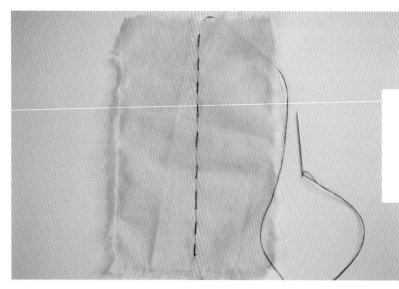

Once you've reached the end of your line, your needle and thread should be on the wrong side of the fabric.

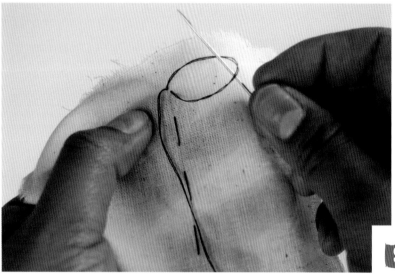

STEP 10

Create a loop and tie to secure, as you did in Steps 4 to 6.

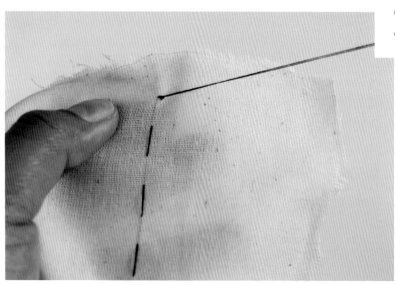

Sewing machine method

Backstitch at the top of the line to lock in your stitches and prevent unraveling, then proceed to stitch all the way along it.

Compare your hand- and machine-sewn samples and continue practicing if needed.

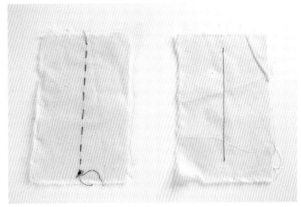

HOW DO I SET MY MACHINE TO BACKSTITCH?

The backstitch control will differ depending on the type of machine you have.

Home machines often have a button that looks like a "U" shape; push it to make the machine stitch backwards.

An industrial machine might have a backstitch lever that you push down as you're sewing.

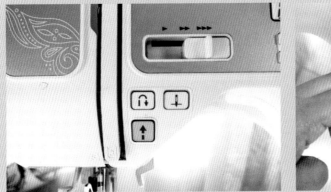

How to clean up raw edges

Sewing machine method

STEP 1

Cut out a square from your scrap fabric.

STEP 2

Set your machine to a zigzag stitch. Use the widest setting with a stitch length of around 1 to 2-½ inches.

STEP 3

Sew along the raw edges of your square.

TIP:

Use the side of the foot as a guide or the sewing gauge built into your machine by matching either along the fabric's raw edge.

Serger method

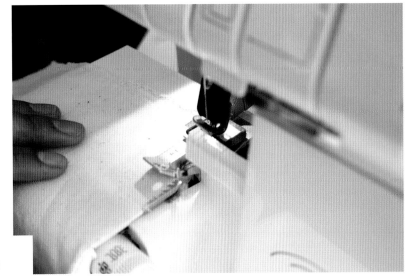

Place your fabric underneath the serger foot, lining it up with the side of your serger.

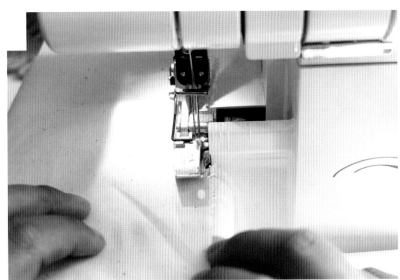

No matter which method you use, they both serve the same purpose: to prevent any fabric from fraying.

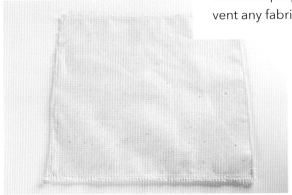

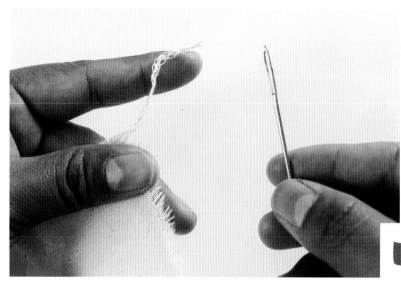

HOW TO HIDE SERGER TAILS

A *serger tail* is the long piece of thread that hangs after you finish serging through your fabric. You can simply cut this thread off, but if you want a cleaner look, follow these steps to hide it.

STEP 1

Choose a hand needle with a large eye.

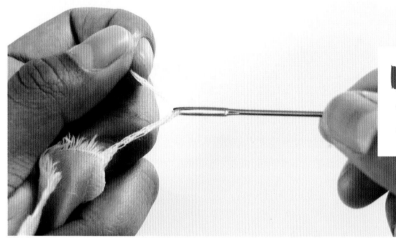

STEP 2

Thread the serger tail through the needle.

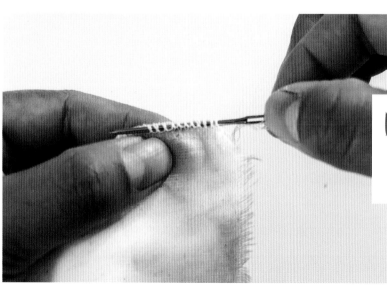

STEP 3

Put your needle through the serger stitches.

STEP 4

Pull the tail all the way through.

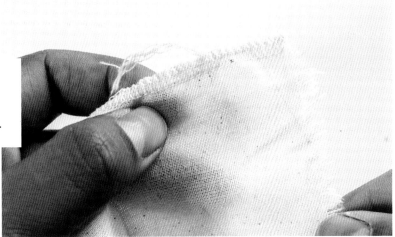

STEP 5

Cut off any excess thread tail.

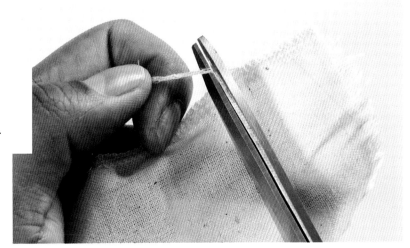

HOW TO SEW A SEAM

STEP 1

Prepare two pieces of fabric.

STEP 2

Serge or zigzag stitch along the raw edges to prevent any fraying.

STEP 3

Place one piece of fabric atop the other with the right sides of the fabric facing together.

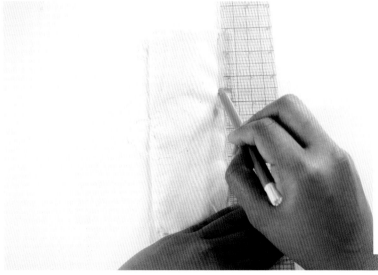

STEP 4

Mark out a *seam allowance* from the edge by drawing a straight line with a ruler ½ inch in from the edge.

TIP:

A seam allowance of ½ inch is standard. Adjust the width if needed for different projects.

STEP 5

Pin your fabric to secure both layers.

TIP:

Pin horizontally instead of vertically so the pins are easier to pull out when sewing on the machine.

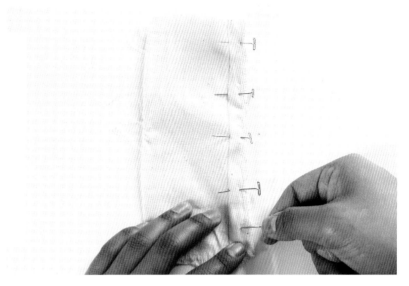

STEP 6

Sew along your marking.

STEP 7

Open the seam with an iron to press the allowance flat.

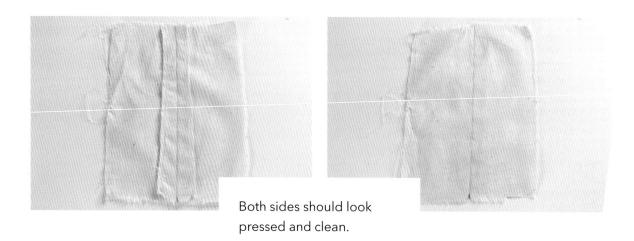

Both sides should look pressed and clean.

HOW TO TOPSTITCH

A *topstitch* is a type of decorative stitch that shows on the right side of fabric. This is common on a lot of heavy-duty fabrics such as denim, canvas, and leather.

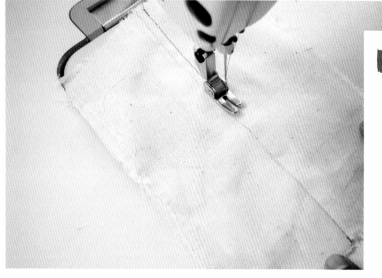

STEP 1

Along a pressed open seam on the right side of fabric, line up the side of your sewing machine's presser foot with the seamline. Sew all the way down.

If you'll be hand sewing, stitch around a ¼ inch from the seamline.

STEP 2

Repeat on the other side of the seam. Don't forget to topstitch on each end to secure the stitches!

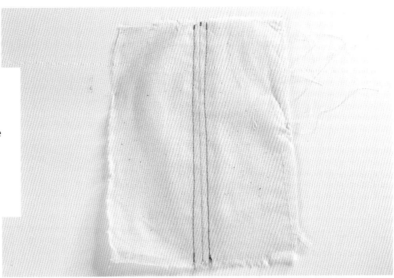

HOW TO SEW A HEM

STEP 1

Prepare your fabric. Cut out a square and serge or zigzag stitch along one raw edge.

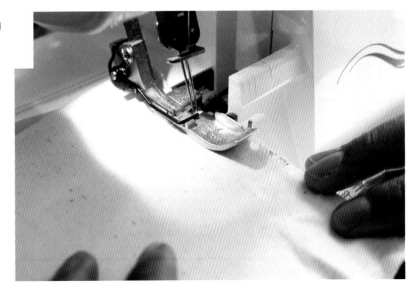

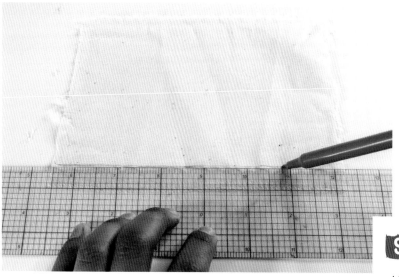

STEP 2

Using a ruler, mark a straight line about ½ inch above and parallel to the finished edge.

STEP 3

Fold your fabric up, following along the marking.

STEP 4

Press down with an iron.

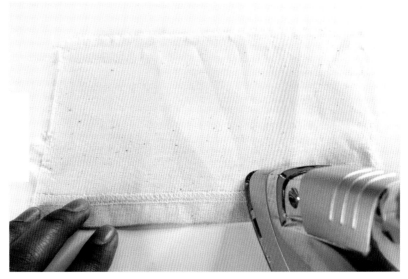

STEP 5

Line up your presser foot with the edge of the fabric and sew to create your hem.

If you're hand sewing, do a running stitch about a ¼ inch away from the serged edge to secure.

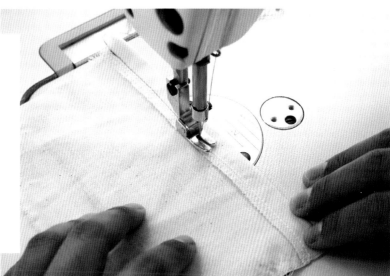

Both sides should look nice and clean!

THE UPCYCLING PROJECTS

PATCHWORK TOP

2 T-shirts

Scissors

Pins

Grid ruler

Marking tool

Iron

Sewing machine or hand-sewing
    supplies

Optional: Serger or overlock
    machine

Estimated time: 30 minutes to
    1 hour

Skill Level: Easy

If you're brand new to upcycling, a patchwork project is one of the easiest to start with. *Patchworking* consists of taking different materials and sewing them together to create one large design. It's a great way to repurpose fabric scraps and unworn clothing items.

You can combine different colors, fabrics, and textures to create a one-of-a-kind look. With more practice, you can even experiment by cutting your pieces into multiple shapes and sizes. The design possibilities are endless!

In this project, I'll show you how to make a checkered top using a basic square patchwork technique and two unworn t-shirts. Because you'll combine half of each t-shirts, you will have enough to make one for yourself and one for a friend!

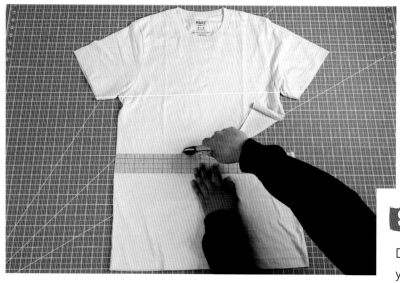

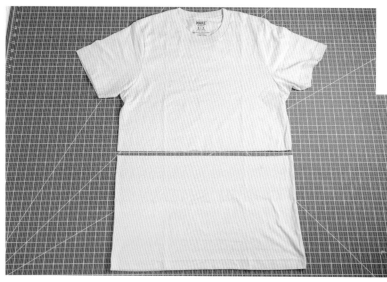

STEP 1

Determine how long you want your finished shirt to be, and then cut your t-shirts to your desired measurements. Factor in a ½-inch seam allowance for the bottom hem.

BEST SHIRT CHOICES

Try to choose t-shirts of similar fabrics for your first patchworking project. Trying to combine a jersey cotton fabric with something silky, for example, can be a bit difficult to maneuver in the machine, especially for beginners.

Likewise, check the size of your t-shirts. If you use shirts that are too tight, you may not have enough space to put your head through the neckline! Try choosing shirts that are a size or two bigger to have more seam allowance to work with.

STEP 2

Lay one t-shirt flat, mark a vertical line down the center of the shirt, and mark another horizontally across the center. Cut along the crossed lines, dividing the shirt into four pieces.

You can play around with the look of your design by cutting the patchwork pieces in different lengths and widths.

Repeat for the other t-shirt.

You now have eight pieces total, four per shirt.

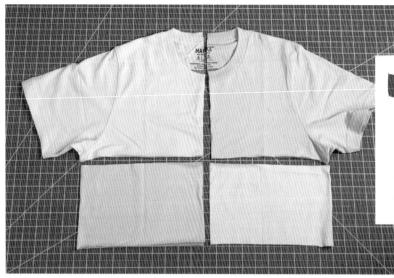

STEP 3

Determine how you want your patchwork design to look, and move each piece into position for the combination you want to achieve.

STEP 4

Pin and sew the front and back vertical seams for the top and bottom halves of the t-shirt.

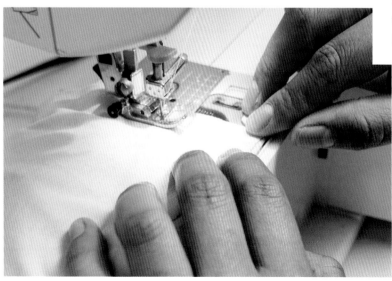

TIP:

If you have a serger, before sewing your pieces together, run any raw edges through the machine to avoid any potential fraying or further stretching of the fabric. Alternatively, you could do a tight zigzag stitch at a 5-width and 1-stitch length along the edges on a home sewing machine.

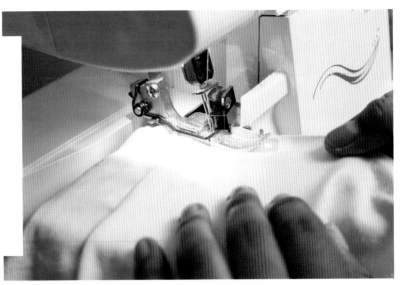

STEP 5

Pin the top and bottom pieces together with the right sides facing each other. Sew to connect the entire t-shirt together.

TIP:

For a seamless patchwork look, match up the vertical seams of the top and bottom pieces, pin them, and sew carefully.

STEP 6

To hem, fold ½ inch inward from the bottom of the t-shirt and sew.

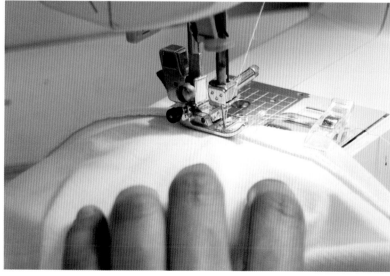

FINAL LOOK

PAINTING DENIM PANTS

WHAT YOU NEED

Denim pants

Acrylic paint

A variety of paint brushes

Marking tool

Disposable tablecloth or
   garbage bag

Cup of water

Paper towels

Iron

Scrap cotton fabric

Cardboard or poster board

Optional: Fabric medium, sticky
   tape, paint palette

Estimated time: 1 day

Skill Level: Easy/Intermediate/
   Advanced, depending on
   your design

If you want to add colors and patterns to a garment without dyeing or using fabric manipulation methods, try painting! Painting is one of the easiest ways to upcycle a garment—without any sewing required! You don't have to be the best artist to create a personal masterpiece that speaks to you.

In this project, you will learn how to paint denim. Come prepared with a design in mind, or freehand lines and shapes!

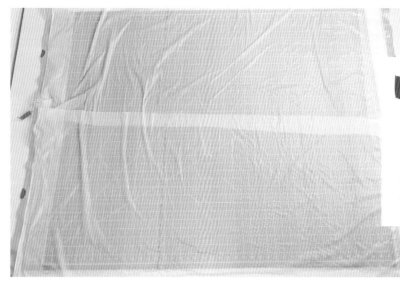

STEP 1

Set up your space. Lay out a disposable tablecloth or garbage bag to reduce mess, and tape it to your painting surface to make sure it doesn't move.

Pour your paint into a palette, set up a cup of water to wet your brushes, and grab some paper towels.

TIP:

If you have a fabric medium available to you, mix it in with your acrylic paint to create the consistency of a fabric paint.

STEP 2

Determine the design you'd like to paint. You can lightly sketch it out first or freehand it with paint but remember that paint is permanent!

STEP 3

Cut out a piece of poster board to place between the fabric layers so the paint doesn't bleed through.

STEP 4

Start painting your design! Take your time, put on a nice show or podcast, and let your creativity flow. Let your pants dry overnight.

TIPS FOR PAINTING

Use a variety of brushes to create different lines and thickness.

For more intricate designs, have thinner paint brushes ready for the smaller details.

For seamless lines and shapes, start with light strokes and move slowly.

Make a mistake? Some designs can be fixed with an ear swab and nail acetone or 91% isopropyl alcohol if the paint is light enough.

Wait for a layer to dry before applying more paint. You don't want the paint to be too thick or it'll feel stiff when it dries.

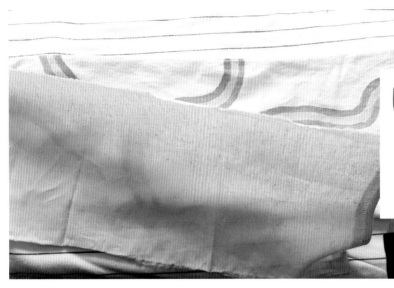

STEP 5

After your pants are completely dry, place a scrap of cotton fabric, such as muslin, over the paint.

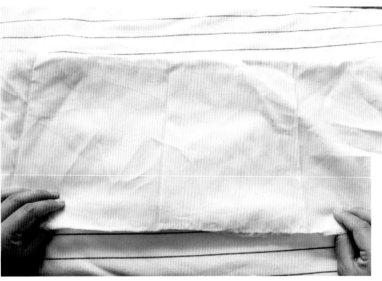

Set your iron on the highest setting with no steam, and slowly iron over each section to heat-set the garment so it doesn't peel or crack the paint.

TIP:

If you don't have an iron, you can also heat-set your garment in a dryer on the highest setting. Don't put any other clothes in with it to avoid color transfer!

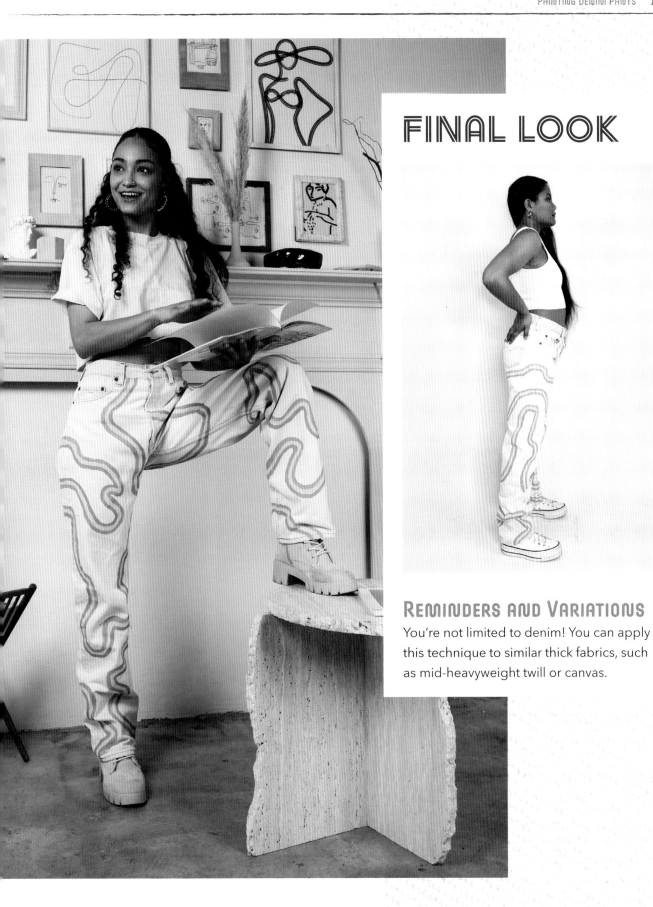

FINAL LOOK

REMINDERS AND VARIATIONS

You're not limited to denim! You can apply this technique to similar thick fabrics, such as mid-heavyweight twill or canvas.

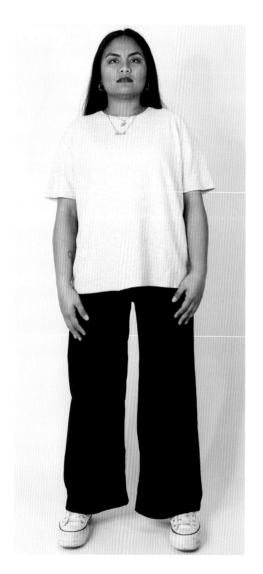

JERSEY T-SHIRT TO TANK TOP

T-shirt

Tank top

Kraft or pattern paper

Paper scissors

Fabric shears

Pencil

Grid ruler

Pins or sewing clips

Sewing machine or hand-sewing supplies

Optional: Serger or overlock machine, French curve ruler

Estimated time: 1 to 2 hours

Skill Level: Easy

TIP:

Try to choose a t-shirt with an ample amount of stretch to it. The stretchier the fabric, the better! By choosing a t-shirt with stretch, you won't have to worry about putting in a set closure such as a zipper.

The best part of upcycling is giving an existing garment new life! Having custom patterns ready to go will allow you to elevate your designs and have any upcycling project fit you better.

In this project, I'll show you how to create a basic pattern from your favorite tank top, then use it to make a new tank top from a t-shirt. Even better: You can use this clothing cloning method not only with tank tops, but with most garments in your closet, as well.

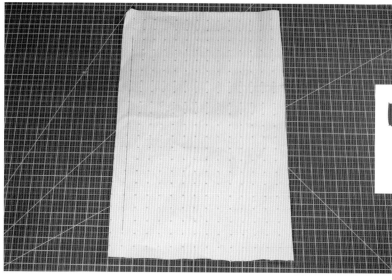

STEP 1

Draw a straight line on the left side of your paper.

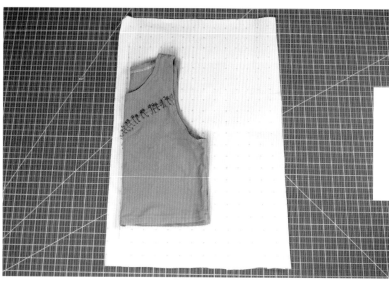

Grab your tank, fold it in half lengthwise with the front facing you, then place the fold along the line you drew.

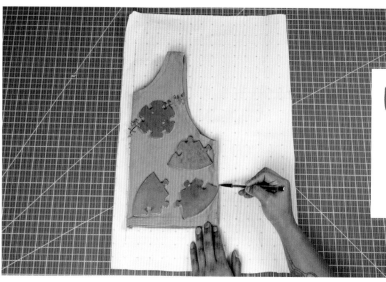

STEP 2

Trace around the tank top. Once you're finished, go over your markings with a ruler for cleaner lines.

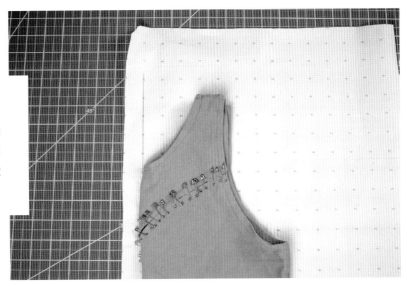

TIP:

When tracing the front side of the tank top, tuck the back neckline out of sight to get the most accurate measurement of the tank.

STEP 3

Draw out a ½-inch seam allowance along the side seam and bottom hem.

For armholes and necklines, draw a ¼-inch seam allowance.

Cut out your front pattern.

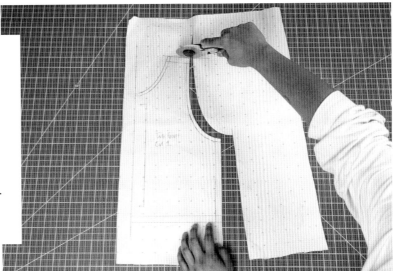

STEP 4

Repeat Steps 1 to 3 to make a pattern for the back of the tank.

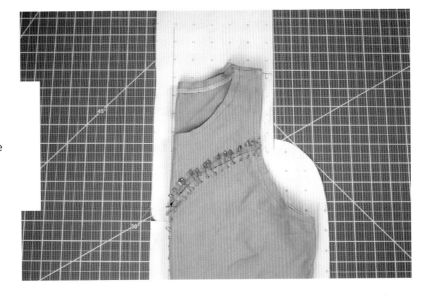

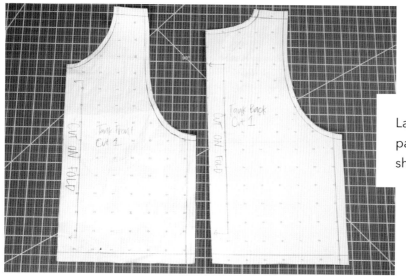

Label your front and back patterns, as well as which side should be placed along a fold.

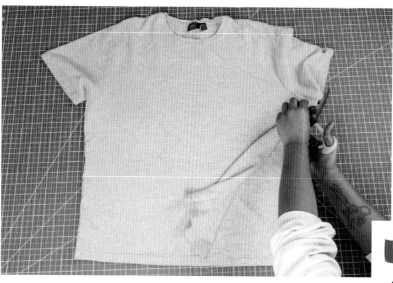

STEP 5

Cut your t-shirt into two pieces along its seams and remove the sleeves the same way.

STEP 6

Fold one t-shirt piece in half horizontally. Place the front pattern's edge on the fold and cut out the front. Repeat with the second t-shirt piece and the back pattern.

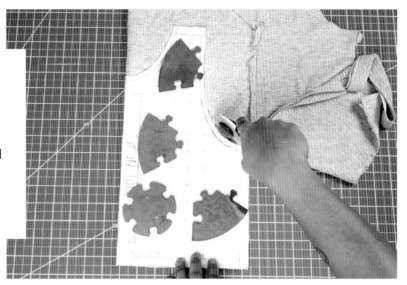

STEP 7

Sew the side and shoulder seams together using a zigzag stitch or stretch stitch on your machine.

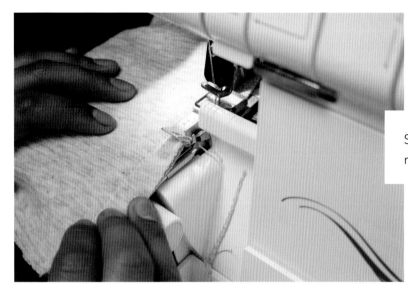

Serge or zigzag stitch any raw edges.

STEP 8

Try on your tank to check the fit. Make any necessary adjustments in the shoulder and side seams.

Hem the neckline, armholes, and bottom of the tank.

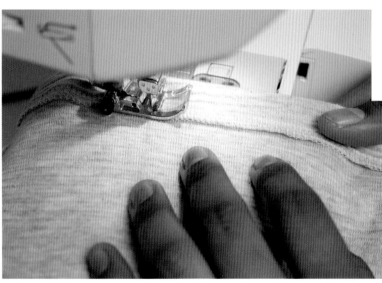

FINAL LOOK

REMINDERS AND VARIATIONS

When creating a clone pattern, you can play around with the design, such as adjusting the length of your tank top or lowering the neckline.

PATCHWORK PANTS

Pants

Fabric or scraps to create a
  patchwork design

Fabric shears

Paper scissors

Seam ripper

Pins or clips

Grid ruler

Marking tool

Pencil

Kraft paper

Sewing machine or hand-sewing
  supplies

Optional: Serger or overlock
  machine

Estimated time: 2 to 6 hours

Skill Level: Intermediate/
  Advanced, depending on
  your design

Patchwork is one of the most popular methods to use when upcycling a garment, offering endless fabric combinations and patchwork designs to choose from! It's a great way to upcycle any fabric scraps from previous projects that you have laying around, too. Experiment with shapes, textures, and stitches for a one-of-a-kind look.

In this project, you will use the technique you learned in the Jersey T-shirt to Tank Top Using the Cloning Method project to modify the shape of your pants, then incorporate a patchwork section made from your fabric scraps of choice.

STEP 1

Lay your pants flat and mark out where you want the patchwork to go.

STEP 2

Cut off each pant leg along your markings.

You now have two pant pieces to use as patterns for the patchwork section.

STEP 3

Using the clothing cloning method, lay the cutoff pant sections flat on the paper and trace around each separately.

Add a ½-inch seam allowance on the top, bottom, and inseam for each piece. You will not need a seam allowance on the outer side of the pattern because you will be placing it on the fold of your fabric. Label your patterns to lessen any confusion during the cutting process!

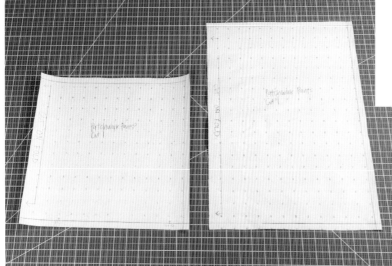

STEP 4

Gather your fabric scraps.

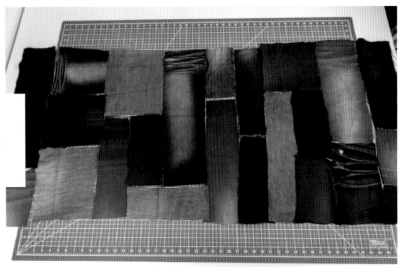

Cut out rectangle and square pieces in a variety of sizes and determine placement.

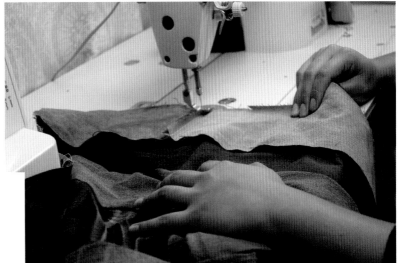

STEP 5

Sew your patchwork fabric together. Fold it in half, and check that both patterns will fit. If they don't, add more pieces to your fabric as needed.

STEP 6

With the fabric folded (right side to right side), place one pattern along the fold and cut. Repeat for the second pattern.

The new pieces will match up to your pant base.

STEP 7

Pin your fabric with right sides together, and sew along the side seam to connect the patchwork fabric into a loop.

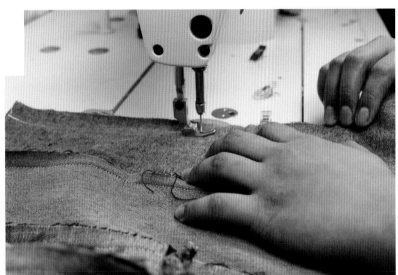

Serge or zigzag stitch any raw edges.

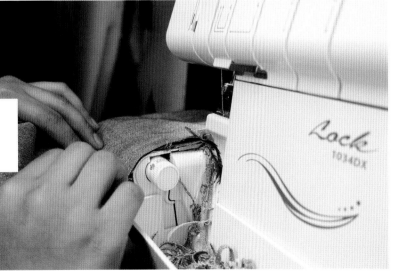

STEP 8

Pin the patchwork pieces to your pants base, with the right sides facing together and raw edges facing down.

Sew along the raw edge to connect all pieces together. At this point, you can hem the bottom of your patchwork pieces for a clean look or leave a frayed hem.

FINAL LOOK

REMINDERS AND VARIATIONS

The longest part of this process is creating the patchwork fabric. Take your time to piece together a patchwork that you'll love!

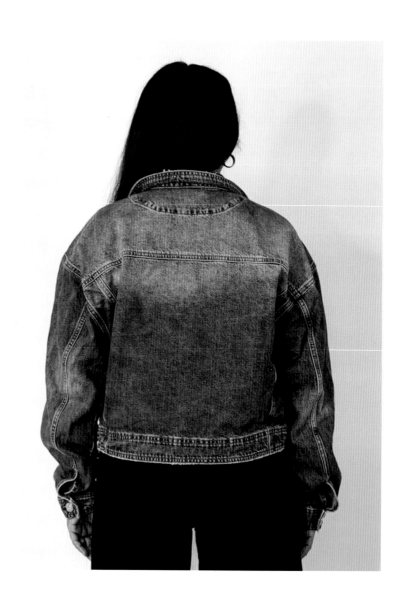

SCRAP FABRIC TO WOVEN-PANEL JACKET

WHAT YOU NEED

Denim jacket

Fabric scraps (enough to cover the entire back section of your jacket)

Fabric shears or rotary cutter

Pins

Sewing machine or hand-sewing supplies

Estimated time: 3 to 5 hours

Skill Level: Intermediate/Advanced

Denim is a necessity in any closet. From frayed cutoff shorts to patchwork floor-length coats, there's a piece out there for everyone. A denim jacket is a seasonless staple that can be worn with many different outfit combinations. You can throw it on over a dress or match it with a pair of pants in the same shade. Decent denim jackets are fairly easy to find secondhand, and they come in so many different washes, silhouettes, and styles!

In this project, I'll show you how to add a woven design detail to your jacket of choice by weaving together upcycled strips of fabric. Denim is one of the most common fabrics to upcycle because of its durability and versatility.

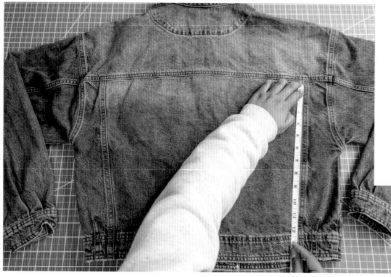

STEP 1

Measure the width and length of your jacket. Determine how wide you want your strips to be and how many rows you want to cover.

The back section of my jacket measured 17 inches wide by 12-½ inches long, so I decided to cut each strip about 2 inches wide to cover the entire back panel. Keep in mind that your numbers may be different from mine, depending on how wide or narrow you want your strips to be.

STEP 2

Create your strips of fabric by cutting or ripping your scraps to your chosen width. You will adjust the lengths later. For now, be sure they're at least long enough to span your jacket's longest dimension.

Always cut some extra strips. It's better to have leftovers than run out in the middle of the project! For my jacket's measurements, I'll need at least 15 of my 2-inch-wide strips.

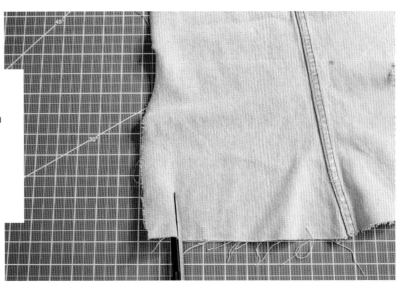

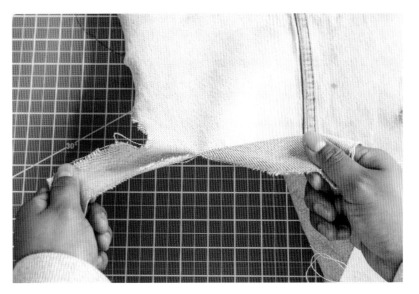

STEP 3

Choose one strip, and fold over one short end by ½ inch (wrong side to wrong side). This is your first vertical strip. Place the folded edge in a top corner of the jacket's back panel, underneath the yoke.

Pin the strip in place (with the right side facing you). Following the line of the yoke, continue to fold and pin the strips right next to each other until you cover the entire section.

STEP 4

Sew across the top of each vertical strip to secure them to the jacket.

STEP 5

Choose your first horizontal strip. Fold over a short end by ½ inch, and then place it along a side panel seam about 1 or 2 inches below the tops of the vertical strips. Pin the folded end in place with the strip laying across the vertical strips.

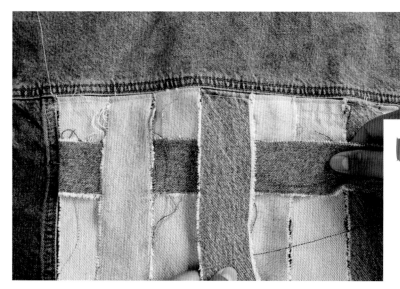

STEP 6

Weave the horizontal strip by going over the first vertical strip, under the second, alternating over and under all the way across.

When you reach the end of the row and the opposite side panel seam, cut any excess fabric from the horizontal strip, leaving a ½-inch hem allowance. Fold under the end, and then pin it to secure the strip's placement.

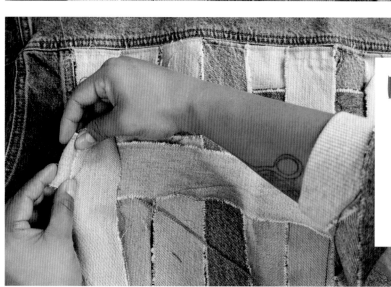

STEP 7

Fold and pin a second horizontal strip right below the first. For this row, start weaving by going under the first vertical strip, then over the second and so on.

Continue adding strips while repeating the weaving pattern until you reach the bottom of the jacket's back panel.

STEP 8

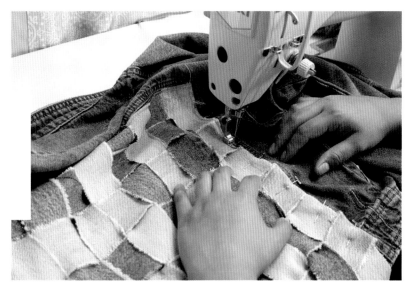

Sew along both ends of the horizontal strips to secure them.

STEP 9

Decide if you want the vertical strips to line up or have different lengths for an uneven, asymmetrical look. Cut each strip to your liking. You can do this now or at the end.

STEP 10

To prevent the weave from shifting, secure the final horizontal strip where it's hidden behind overlapping vertical strips. Fold the vertical strip out of the way, pin that section of the horizontal strip in place and sew in that area to secure it. Flip the vertical strip back in place to hide the stitches. Repeat across the row.

FINAL LOOK

REMINDERS AND VARIATIONS

Try combining different shades of denim for a multicolored woven look—make a pattern or embrace randomness. If you don't want fraying edges, you can zigzag stitch or hem each strip.

CREATING A LACE-UP GARMENT

Garment of choice

Eyelets

Eyelet kit (consists of an eyelet setter and anvil) or eyelet press

Hammer

Fabric shears, fabric snips, or punch

Trimming for drawstring

Grid ruler

Marking tool

Estimated time: 1 to 2 hours
Skill Level: Easy/Intermediate

When you're upcycling, it can feel overwhelming to decide on the right fastening option for your design. From exposed zippers to colorful snaps, the fastener can instantly change how the finished project turns out. Lace-up details are not only distinctive fasteners, but also great decorative elements. You run lace-up details down a jacket's sleeves, curve them around the legs of your pants, or ring the neckline of a t-shirt.

In this project, I'll show you how to add a stylistic twist to any garment by adding eyelets for a lace-up effect.

STEP 1

Choose your eyelets and decide where you want to add them on your garment. I decided to add the eyelets as a closure along the front of a cut jacket that I turned into a top.

STEP 2

Mark your holes about 1 inch apart from each other.

Create a small snip at the markings with scissors or a punch. Make it big enough for the eyelet to go through.

STEP 3

There are two parts of an eyelet. The longer part is the shank, while the smaller part is the washer.

Insert the eyelet with the long shank through the hole, from the right side of the fabric. Put the washer through the wrong side of the fabric and the eyelet.

STEP 4

Set an eyelet using the method of your choice.

STEP 5

Repeat until all eyelets are set, and thread through your trimming.

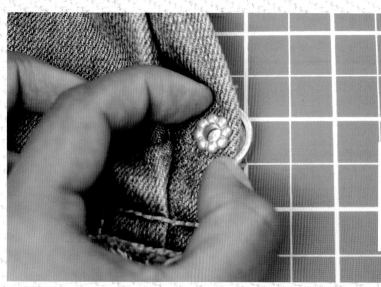

How to Set an Eyelet

Option 1: Eyelet setter and anvil

STEP 1

Place the eyelet on top of the setter.

STEP 2

From the right side of the fabric, insert the anvil and lightly tap it with a hammer a few times.

Option 2: Eyelet press

STEP 1

Put your fabric between the jaws of the eyelet press.

STEP 2

Clamp the press down to insert the eyelets.

FINAL LOOK

REMINDERS AND VARIATIONS

Eyelets come in a variety of colors, shapes, and sizes, so they can add a pop of personality or blend into the background of your design. If you'll be inserting eyelets regularly, investing in an eyelet press might be a worthwhile option.

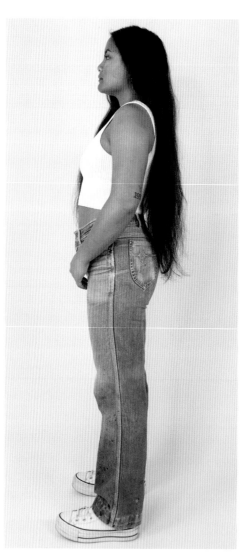

PANT LEGS TO PLEATED SKIRT

WHAT YOU NEED

Pants

Fabric shears

Pins or clips

Grid ruler

Marking tool

Sewing machine or hand-sewing supplies

Iron

Optional: Serger or overlock machine

Estimated time: 2 to 3 hours

Skill Level: Advanced

TIP:

Choose pants that fit you nicely on the waist for minimal alterations.

Pleated skirts aren't meant to be worn only with school uniforms or for afternoon tennis matches. Pair one with a chunky sweater and knee-high boots for a fall outfit or your favorite t-shirt and sneakers when running your day-to-day errands. Now that you know how to turn pants into a skirt, you can experiment with creating different designs! In this project, you'll build on the skills you learned in the Pants to Skirt project and transform pant legs into pleats.

STEP 1

Determine the length you want the yoke of your skirt to be. I recommend extending it about 1 to 2 inches below the zipper fly for an average length. Mark a line, then cut across both legs.

If you cut above the crotch seam, continue to Step 2. If you chose a longer yoke seam, rip and sew as you did in Steps 2 to 5 and Step 7 in the Pants to Skirt project.

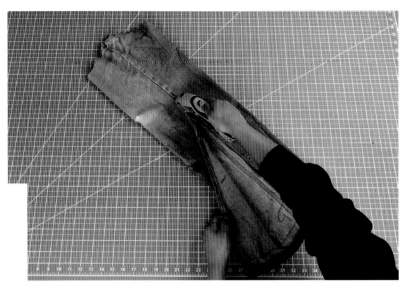

STEP 2

Snip the pant legs apart at the crotch, if necessary. Open one leg's side seam to make a single continuous panel, then open (or cut next to) the leg's other seam to split the panel in half.

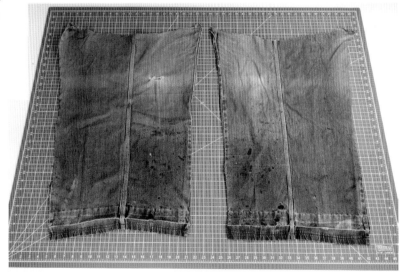

Repeat for the second leg. You now have four panels total.

If you want your pleats to be a certain length, cut and adjust the panels to match.

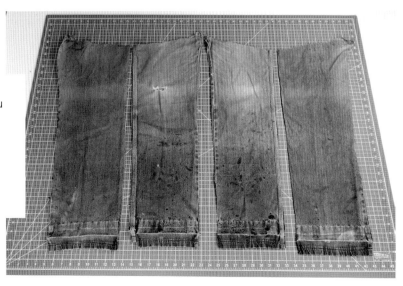

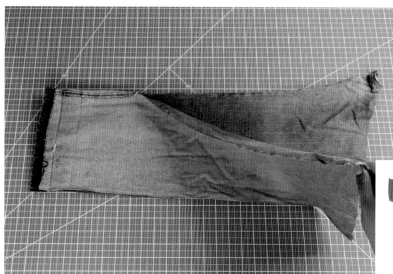

STEP 3

You're going to be sewing the panels together short end to short end to create a long narrow strip. First, make sure all your panels are the same size and adjust as needed. Stacking them and cutting once through several layers is a quick way to do this.

STEP 4

Place two panels right sides together and sew along the side (short) seam. Place the third panel right sides together with the second, pin, and sew. Add the fourth panel the same way, if needed.

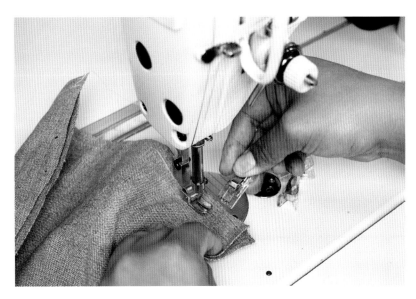

STEP 5

You now have one continuous strip. Serge or zigzag stitch along the raw long edges. If you'd prefer a frayed hem, serge or zigzag only the top long edge.

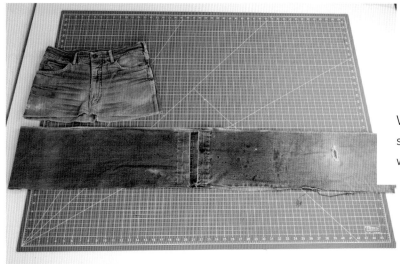

When folded in half, the strip should be double or triple the width of your skirt.

STEP 6

Mark a ½-inch seam allowance on one of the short ends. Turn the strip right sides together and sew the ends closed to make a loop.

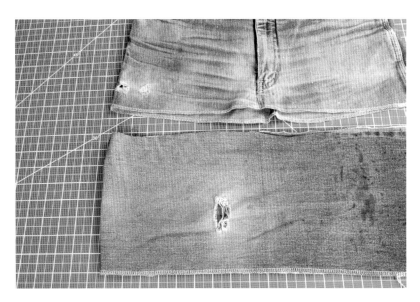

STEP 7

With the right side out and starting at a seam, begin making loosely folded pleats. They don't have to be super close together, just enough to where it can fit around the entire width of the skirt!

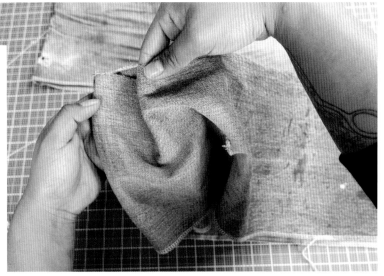

If this is your first time making a pleat, follow these steps to create a simple knife pleat:

- Make a mark 1 inch away from the edge

- Make a second marking about 2 inches away from the first mark.

- Pinch over the second marking to the first, so that they match.

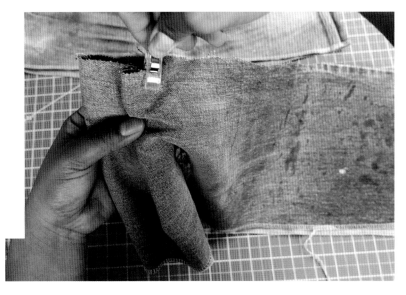

Pin and repeat!

Hold each pleat in place by pinning or clipping the folds together at the top and bottom. Continue pleating around the entire loop. When you finish, check that the pleated loop matches the width of your skirt base. Adjust the pleats if needed.

STEP 8

Along the top edge of the loop, sew on the right side (going with the direction of the folds) to secure the pleats.

STEP 9

To connect the pleats to your skirt base, put the right sides facing together. Match the sewn edge of the pleated panel with the skirt base's raw edge, pin, and sew.

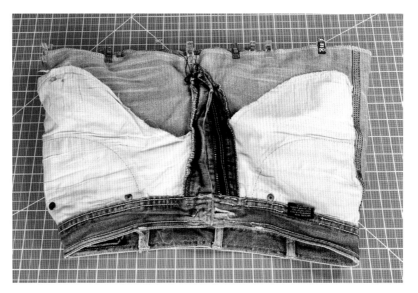

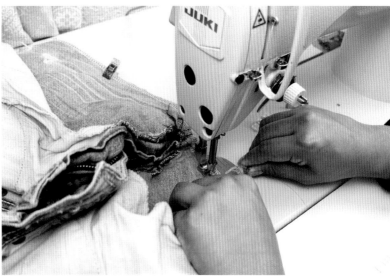

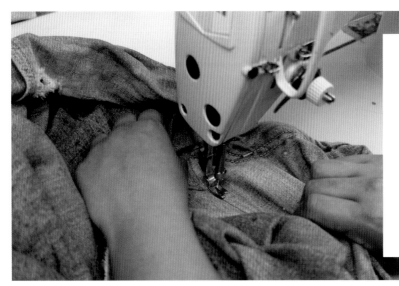

Turn the skirt right side out.

On the right side of the fabric, you can top stitch along the seam where the skirt base and pleats meet. This adds a decorative element while also securing the seam allowance to the inside of the skirt, making it more comfortable to wear.

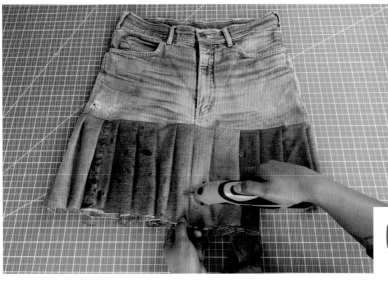

STEP 10

Remove the pins or clips at the hemline, shorten any pleats if needed, and press them with an iron for a cleaner look.

FINAL LOOK

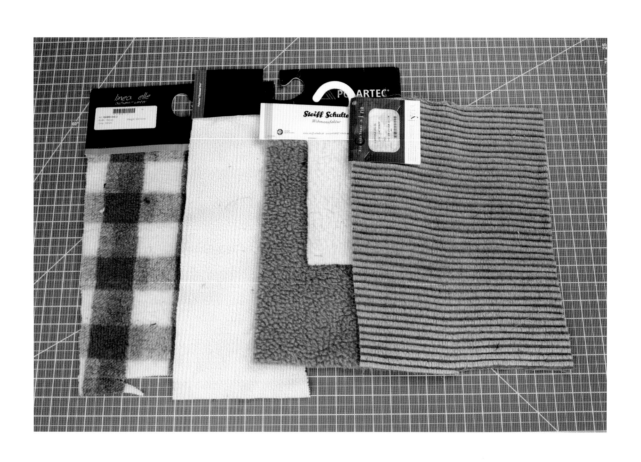

FABRIC SCRAPS TO KNOT BAG

WHAT YOU NEED

Scrap fabrics or linens

Fabric shears

Pins or clips

Grid ruler

Patternmaking or kraft paper

Marking tool

Sewing machine or hand-sewing supplies

Optional: Serger or overlock machine

Estimated time: 1 to 2 hours

Skill Level: Easy

TIP:

Choose sturdy, durable fabrics help the bag hold its shape.

Knot bags were made popular in Japan to hold small items or wrap gifts. A knot bag consists of two asymmetrical handles, with one handle going through the other, creating the knot effect. With its simple yet functional silhouette, it's the perfect bag choice if you need to securely hold your belongings while still bringing in a fashionable twist. Incorporate it into an outfit for a night out or design a personalized bag to give to friends or family.

In this tutorial, you will be using scrap fabrics or linens to create a one-of-a-kind knot bag.

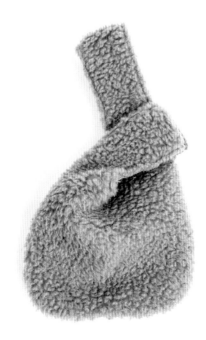

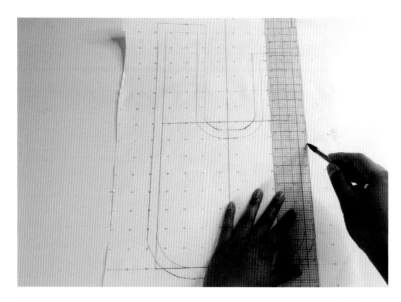

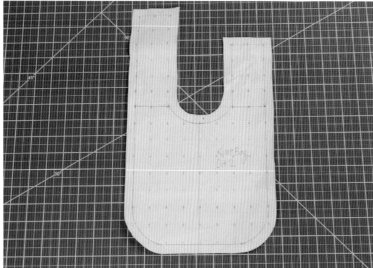

STEP 1

Make a pattern for your small knot bag:

1. Draw an 8x8-inch square (the body), then a straight, vertical line down its center.

2. From the top-right of the square, draw a 4-inch high, 2-inch-wide rectangle (the first handle).

3. At the top-left of the square, draw an 6x2-inch rectangle.

4. Round off the bottom corners of the square.

5. Mark 1 inch down the body's center line, and draw a curve through this point that connects the inner edges of the handles

6. Add a ½-inch seam allowance all the way around and cut out the pattern.

STEP 2

Pin the pattern to a piece of fabric from your scraps (right side up), and cut out the bag's first side.

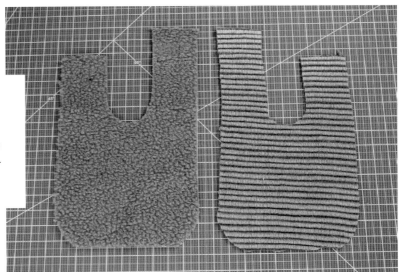

Flip the pattern over, pin it to your second piece of fabric's right side, and cut. This makes sure that the pieces will mirror each other.

STEP 3

Serge or zigzag stitch around the raw edges.

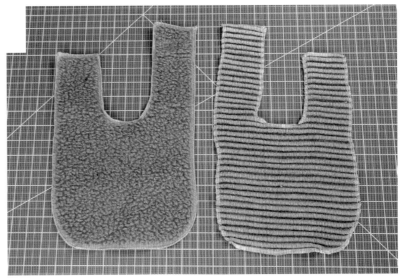

STEP 4

On each side of the bag, mark about ½ inch down from the top of the body (base of the handles).

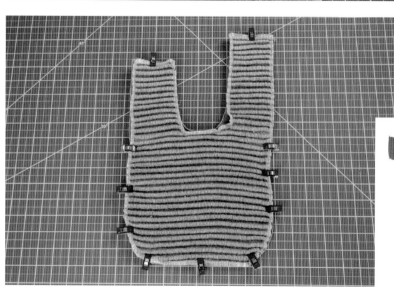

STEP 5

With the right sides of the fabric facing each other, sew the handles together at the top. Next, sew the bag's body from one of the side marks, around the base to the other mark.

STEP 6

Flip your bag right-side out.

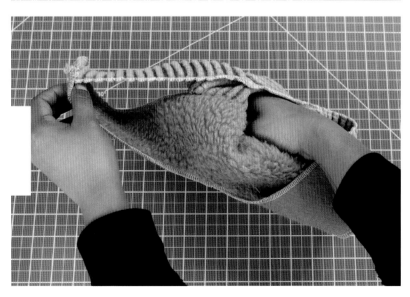

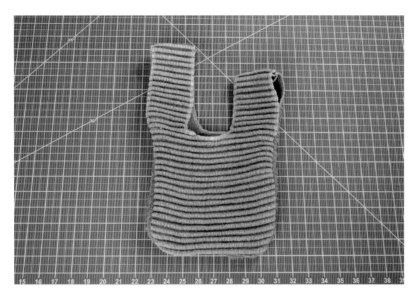

Fold, pin, and sew along the handles' open edges to create a ¼-inch hem.

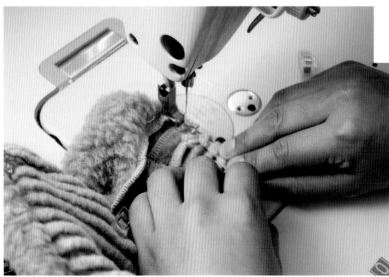

FINAL LOOK

REMINDERS AND VARIATIONS
Customize the shape of the bag and its handles to make it bigger!

ADJUSTABLE DRAWSTRING BUTTON-UP

WHAT YOU NEED

Button-up shirt (or any top of your choice)

Fabric shears

Grid ruler

French curve ruler

Pins or clips

Chalk or water-soluble marker

Matching trimming (ribbon, string, elastic cording, etc.)

Safety pin

Sewing machine or hand-sewing supplies

Optional: Serger or overlock machine

Estimated time: 1 hour

Skill Level: Intermediate

TIP:

Choose a top that isn't too short or cropped for better results.

One way to make the most out of your sewing and upcycling projects is to add a functional design element. It can be as simple as choosing a separating zipper or more complex like adding snaps to your pant legs so they can turn into shorts. An easy way to incorporate functionality without sacrificing style is by adding drawstrings. With these, you can adjust the length of any garment you desire.

In this project, we'll be upcycling an unworn button-up shirt into a double drawstring top, adding one on each side at the waist. You'll be able to style this button up in multiple ways and customize it to match your personal style.

STEP 1

Lay the shirt flat. Determine how far beneath the armholes you want your drawstrings to run. Use the ruler to mark the spots; I put mine just a few inches underneath each armhole. With the French curve, draw matching curves, one down each side from your mark to the shirt's hem.

STEP 2

Cut along the curve through both layers of shirt at the same time.

Zigzag stitch or serge along the raw edges to prevent fraying.

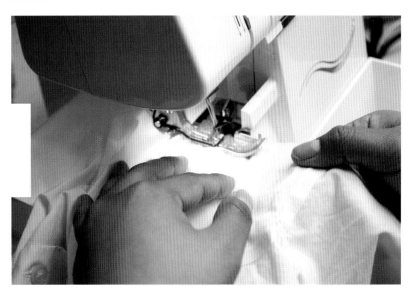

STEP 3

Create the channel for your drawstrings. Starting at the front of the shirt's hem, make a ½-inch to 1-inch fold to the inside and pin, continuing up under the armhole and down to the back's hem.

Repeat for the second curve.

Sew the curves.

TIP:

Sewing curves can be a bit tricky. Be sure to use enough pins or clips so that the seam is held down nicely!

STEP 4

Cut out two pieces of your trimming to use as draw-strings. Make them long enough to thread through the entire channel, plus a few inches extra. For the example, I used an elastic stretch cord.

STEP 5

Connect a safety pin at one end of a drawstring, then insert it into one of the channels to begin threading it through.

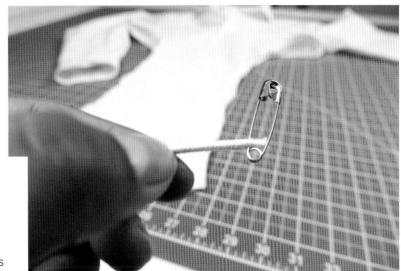

TIP:

If you prefer, you can use a loop turner to thread the drawstrings through the channels instead.

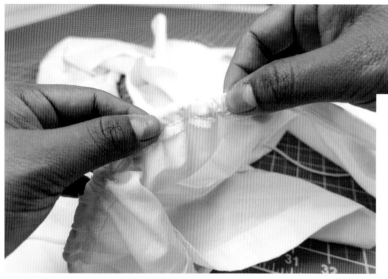

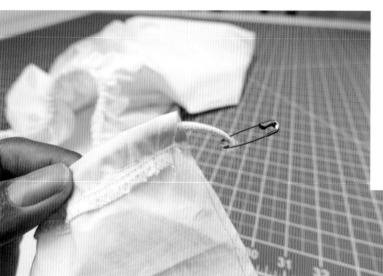

STEP 6

Push the safety pin all the way through until you get to the end.

TIP:

With synthetic drawstring or trimming such as elastic cording, you can lightly burn the ends to prevent fraying.

STEP 7

Secure each drawstring with a knot or cord lock. Repeat for both sides of the top.

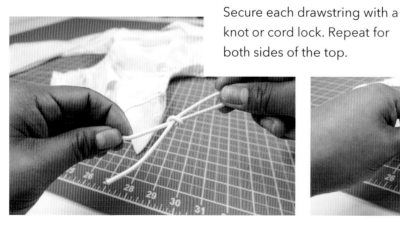

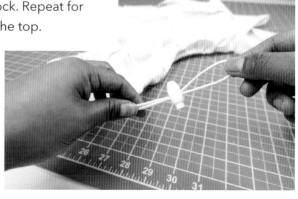

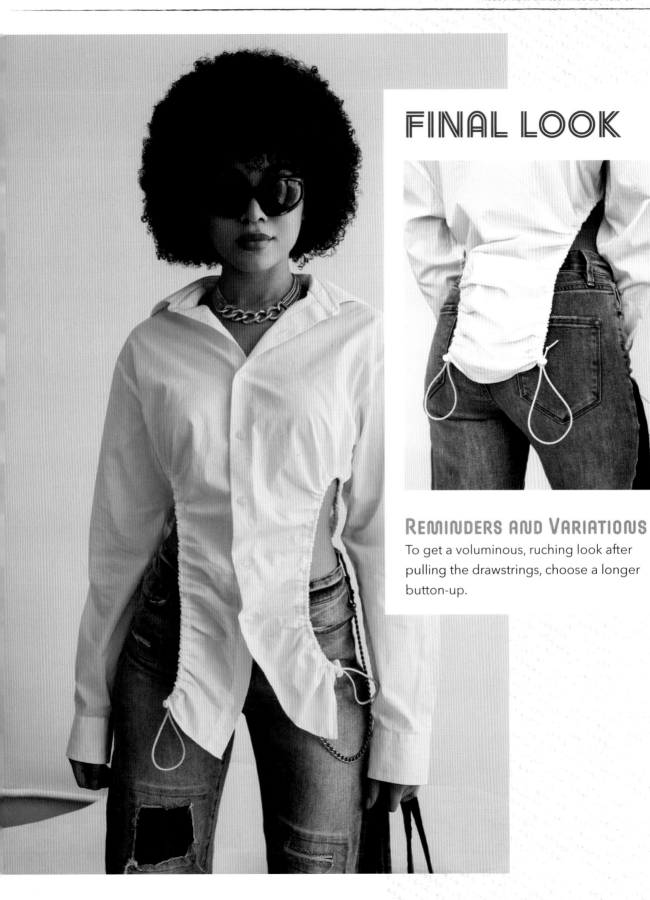

FINAL LOOK

REMINDERS AND VARIATIONS

To get a voluminous, ruching look after pulling the drawstrings, choose a longer button-up.

SKINNY JEANS TO WIDE-LEG PANTS

Skinny jeans

Extra fabric for flare panels

Fabric shears

Seam ripper

Pins or clips

Grid ruler

Marking tool

Sewing machine or hand-sewing supplies

Optional: Serger or overlock machine

Estimated time: 2 hours

Skill Level: Intermediate

TIP:

For the panels, choose any fabric that speaks to you! You can match the color of your pants for a cohesive, subtle look, or go bold by choosing a contrasting fabric.

A statement piece for any outfit, pants come in silhouettes for any occasion. Getting ready for a hip-hop class? Choose baggy sweatpants to move more freely. Going to a 1970s-themed event? Corduroy bell bottoms could be an option. Taking a beachside stroll during a tropical vacation? Palazzo pants are a great choice. Not only is there a silhouette out there for everyone, but you can also transform one into another with upcycling.

In this project, I'll show you how to convert a pair of skinny jeans into wide-leg pants by adding in flares. You can use this technique on any pair of pants, shorts, or bottoms that you want to add a flare to.

STEP 1

Mark where you want the flare to start. Try on the pants if needed. I chose a point on the outseam a few inches below the waistband.

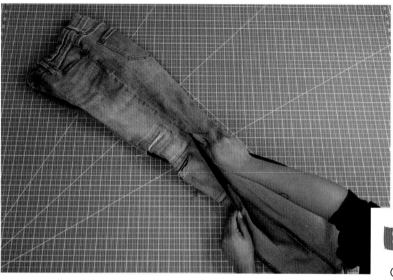

STEP 2

On both legs, seam rip the outseam up to your mark. You can stitch back and forth at the end to secure it.

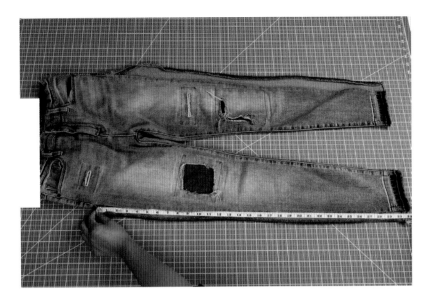

STEP 3

Measure the length of the opening.

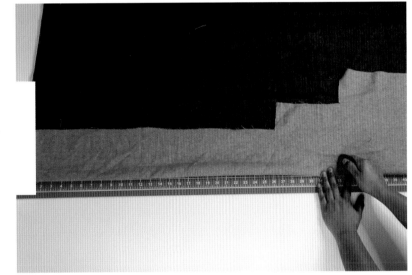

Fold your flare fabric in half (right sides facing), measure out the opening length, and mark the fabric.

STEP 4

Determine your flare's desired width. For a subtle look, keep the widest point less than 4 inches. If you want something dramatic, go as big as you want! At the bottom of your length measurement, measure out half your desired width (remember the fabric is folded) and mark the point.

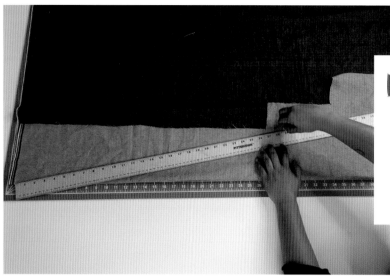

STEP 5

Create a triangle by drawing a line from the width mark (the base) angling up to the top of your length measurement (the point).

Add lines ½ inch from and parallel to your triangle's angled line and base to account for the seam allowance and a hem.

Cut along these new lines,
then serge or zigzag stitch any
raw edges.

TIP:

Hem the bottom of the flare pieces or
leave it frayed before connecting onto
your main pant base. You can omit
adding a hem allowance if you'd prefer
a frayed bottom on your flare.

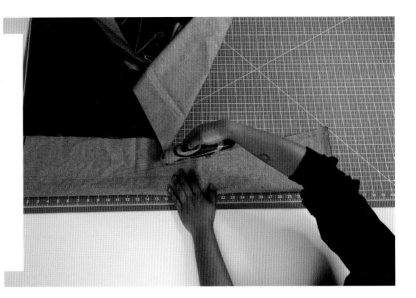

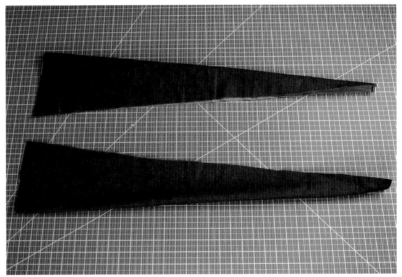

STEP 6

Position your pants with one open side facing up. Place your flare underneath the opening (right side out) and pin the pants on top, staring at the hip/flare tip and matching along the flare's angle down the leg. Repeat for the second leg.

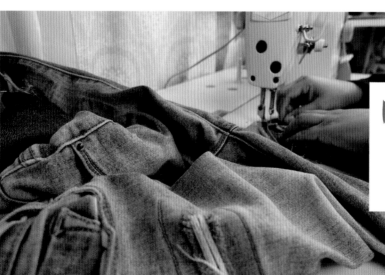

STEP 7

Sew along the edge of the pants to connect everything together.

FINAL LOOK

BLAZER TO TWO-PIECE SET

Blazer

Fabric shears

Seam ripper

Pins or clips

Buttons or snaps

Grid ruler

Marking tool

Sewing machine or hand-sewing supplies

Optional: Serger or overlock machine, extra lace fabric or trimming

Estimated time: 2 to 3 hours

Skill Level: Intermediate

TIP:

When choosing a blazer, select one with a looser fit to the body. During the upcycling process, you'll be moving around the fabric to your liking and this will leave room for mistakes or fit adjustments.

Many people tend to think that blazers are only for business attire or a special event because of their structured appearance. Over the years, however, blazer styling has been redefined and deconstructed for modern wearers. Style a blazer with a t-shirt, jeans, and sneakers for a casual on-the-go look, or pair one with a mini-skirt, blouse, and lace-up heels for an elevated date night outfit. Or turn one into something entirely new! In this project, I'll show you how to turn a blazer into a matching two-piece set that you can wear together or separately.

STEP 1

Lay your blazer flat and determine where you want to divide it into its jacket and skirt portions. I recommend going a few inches under the armhole. Cutting below the lapels will make sewing easier, too.

Mark a guideline, adding a ½-inch seam allowance to your desired jacket length.

TIP:

Keep in mind that the closer you mark toward the armhole, the more cropped your blazer will turn out to be. Try on your blazer after marking and throughout the process to examine the fit.

STEP 2

Cut through both layers of the blazer along your guideline.

STEP 3

Pin and hem both cut edges: the bottom of the jacket and at the skirt's waistline.

To create a clean hem with no visible raw edges, fold in your lining and outer fabric individually at a ½-inch hem allowance. Pin both layers together to match, then sew along the edge to catch both fabrics in the same sewing pass.

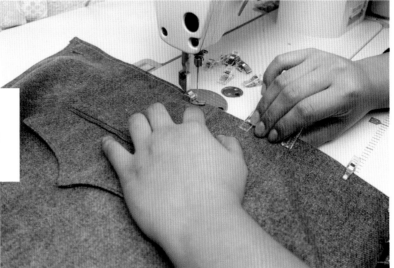

Once you've sewn the jacket hem, half of your two-piece set is finished!

STEP 4

On the skirt portion, if your blazer has any vents at the back, pin and sew them closed.

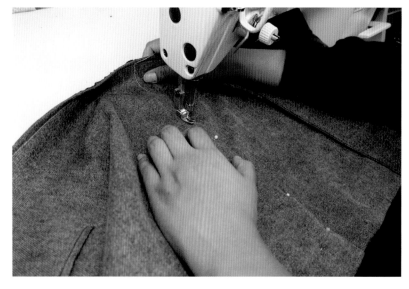

STEP 5

Try on the skirt portion or put it around a dress form. Mark through the buttonholes where you want your new closure to be. If the fabric piece is long, overlap the ends for a wrap-skirt look.

TIP:

If the skirt portion turns out to be too short, you can sew on an additional layer along the bottom hem that complements your fabric, such as adding lace or a fun trim. This is an easy way to add onto the design.

STEP 6

Remove any buttons from the skirt portion and resew them at your new closure markings.

How to Sew a Button

STEP 1

Grab a needle, thread that matches your garment, and your button.

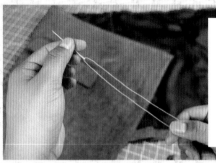

STEP 2

Thread your needle. To make sure you have enough thread, cut it at about arm's length. Double up on the thread for durability.

STEP 3

With your thread and needle, create a knot at the mark your made at the button's new location.

STEP 4

Put the needle through the button's hole and start sewing in and out of the fabric a few times.

STEP 5

To secure your button, create one last knot by tying it off like in Step 3 and cutting off any excess thread.

FINAL LOOK

REMINDERS AND VARIATIONS

If you don't like the blazer's original buttons, change them to fit your personality. Or, you can replace the buttons entirely with a snap closure.

  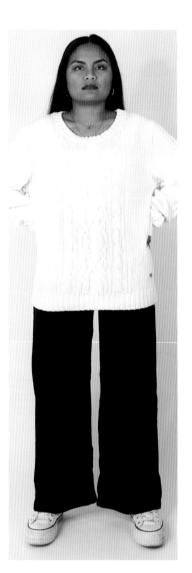 

KNIT SWEATER SWEATSHIRT DUO

Knit sweater

Sweatshirt

Pins

Grid ruler

French curve ruler

Marking tool

Sewing machine or hand-sewing supplies

Optional: Serger or overlock machine

Estimated time: 2 to 3 hours

Skill Level: Intermediate

In fashion, there are many ways to show off your personal style. One way to stand out is to do the unexpected. You could play around with color blocking and prints, wear chunky jewelry, or walk around in the highest platform boots. When it comes to an upcycling project, incorporating a juxtaposition of two fabrics into one design is a guaranteed way to have your finished product feel one of a kind.

In this project, you will learn how to cut and combine two garments together without a pattern and sew along the curvy style lines that you've created. You are also going to complete two garments at once!

STEP 1

Determine your main and secondary garment. Lay your main garment flat. On it, mark out a curvy line where the two will eventually join.

STEP 2

Carefully cut both layers of the garment, following your curvy line while leaving a ½-inch seam allowance.

STEP 3

With the main curved piece cut out, place the other section of the main garment on top of the secondary garment to act as a pattern. Because I wanted the sweater as the upper part of my finished top, I used the lower portion of the sweater as a pattern for the sweatshirt.

Cut the secondary garment, following along the main garment's curves and factoring in a ½-inch seam allowance.

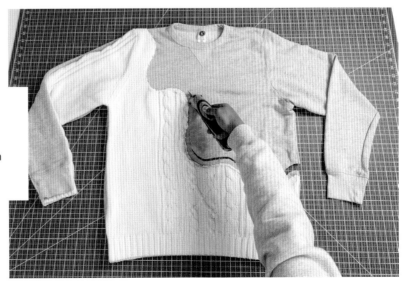

Both pieces should line up and fit along each other. Serge or zigzag stitch any raw edges.

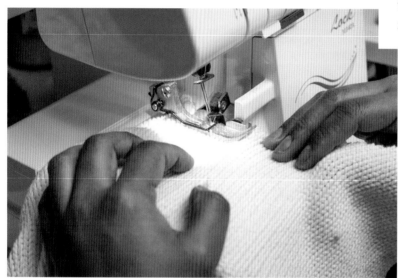

STEP 4

Once you have all your pieces, place the cut secondary garment on top of the main garment. Slightly overlap the curves so it matches the ½- inch seam allowance. The main garment piece should basically be sandwiched between the front and back of the secondary garment piece. Pin generously.

Carefully sew with a zigzag or stretch stitch to connect all pieces together. Pay attention to your seam allowance measurement and stop every few stitches to assure that both layers are getting sewn through.

TIP:

Sewing curves can be a bit tricky. Be sure to use enough pins or clips so that the seams are held down nicely! For a cleaner seam, face your garments right sides together and the seam allowance edges lined up, and then sew.

You can stop here, or further elevate your design by weaving yarn throughout the knit section of your new garment.

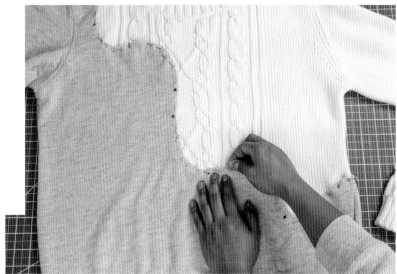

STEP 5

With yarn and a darning needle, weave pieces of cut yarn through your knitwear to add a pop of color.

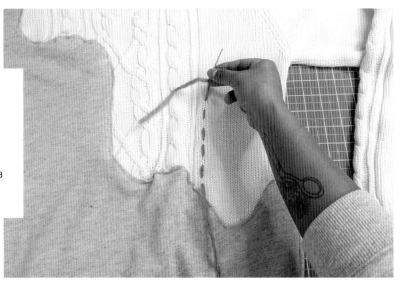

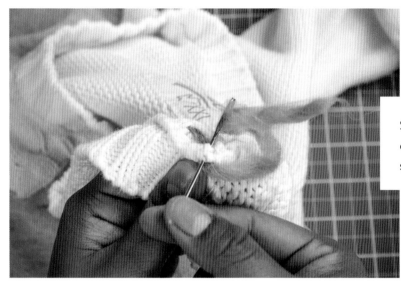

Secure its ends by tying a knot on the inside of the sweater's shoulder seam.

FINAL LOOK

REMINDERS AND VARIATIONS

With the leftover pieces, you can sew them together to create a second garment.

Choose a sweatshirt and sweater that are similar in size and proportions to ensure a better fit on you. For example, pairing a small sweatshirt with an XL knit sweater won't match up accurately when cutting out your curved pieces.

NECKTIES TO SKIRT

A variety of ties (enough to go around your hips or waist; probably 12 or more)

Skirt or shorts for reference

Fabric shears

Measuring tape

Pins or clips

Zipper of choice (invisible or regular)

Sewing machine or hand-sewing supplies

Iron

Optional: Serger or overlock machine, hook and eye

Estimated time: 3 to 6 hours

Skill Level: Advanced

Neckties are an accessory that may feel like you can wear them on specific occasions only, just like ski masks and Santa hats. Coming in a wide array of patterns, colors, and sizes, neckties act as statement pieces, matching a wearer's personality and outfit of the day. You can find neckties at many secondhand shops and thrift stores, with no two ties ever matching. From an upcycler's perspective, they're a wonderful opportunity for a challenge.

In this project, I'll show you how to turn a tangle of ties into a functional skirt. Along the way, you'll learn how to insert a zipper closure in a garment, as well.

STEP 1

Lay out your ties to get a sense of which you might want next to which in your skirt, as well as their general shapes. Most ties start thin on one end, and gradually taper out wider to their tip.

STEP 2

Decide where you'd want your skirt to sit on your body and its length. For reference, place a skirt or pair of shorts that fit you well on top of your ties to roughly determine how many you'll need.

Cut the ties to your desired skirt length, factoring in seam allowance and room for any mistakes.

In this example, I used a skirt I already had as a reference to figure out the length I want to cut my ties at. I cut the ties about a ½ inch above the waistband of my skirt.

STEP 3

Starting with a tie you want on your hip, pin or clip the first two ties together along their adjacent edges and with right sides facing each other. Add the third tie in your front design to the second in the same way and continue this way across the skirt to the tie for the opposite hip.

TIP:

Wrap the ties around your body every few sections to check the fit. The length at the top should match your waist or hips measurement, with an additional few inches for leeway and the zipper seams.

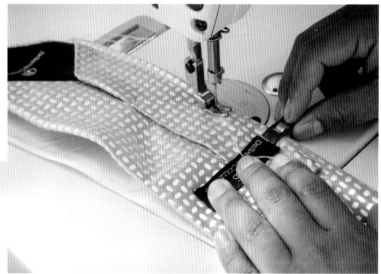

STEP 4

Sew the pinned tie edges together to form the front of the skirt.

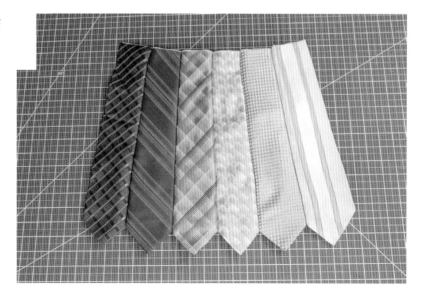

STEP 5

For the back part of the skirt, separate your ties evenly, with a middle section open for the zipper. Repeat Steps 4 and 5 to connect the back ties together into the two sections that will go on either side of the zipper. Do *not*, however, attach the ties on either side of the zipper gap to each other. You'll attach those to the zipper later instead.

STEP 6

Place the front and back pieces of the skirt right sides together. Pin or clip the sides to sew.

Check the skirt's fit and add or subtract any ties as needed. Serge or zigzag stitch along the top of the ties to avoid any fraying edges.

STEP 7

From the leftover skinny ends of your neckties, choose one (or several) to use as the skirt's waistband. Measure out its length along the skirt top. Trim it if necessary or stitch two or more together if you need something a bit longer.

STEP 8

Pin the waistband to the skirt with right sides facing right together and sew.

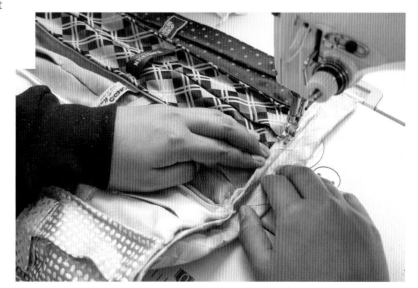

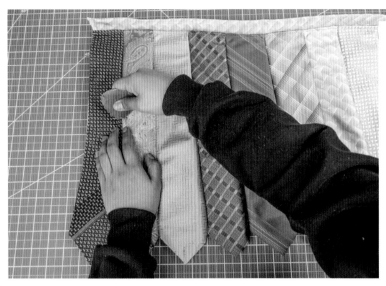

STEP 9

Just like the Skinny Jeans to Flared Pants project, we're going to add a flare in between the ties to make the skirt fit better along your hips. In this example, I'll be adding them into the back section of the skirt, but you can choose to add this anywhere you'd like.

Starting at one side of the back section of the skirt, mark a few inches up from the bottom of the skirt.

STEP 10

Seam rip all the way up to the mark between two ties. Sew above the seam ripped opening to secure the end so the opening doesn't rip through.

STEP 11

Find a skinny end amongst the excess cut ties that you think will look good in the gap you just created. This will act as the flare in the skirt. Cut this piece slightly longer than the gap but have the point of the tie match up with the rest of the ties.

Place the new tie piece underneath the opening, and pin along the edges (wrong side of the main ties to right side of the flare) to the ties on either side. Sew it in place on the right side of the skirt.

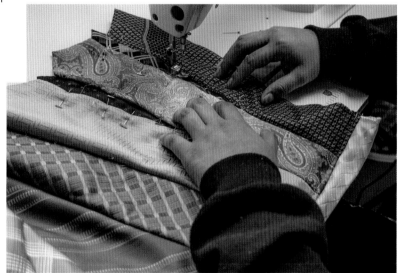

You can repeat this throughout the entire skirt, or just add flares between the ties in the two back sections.

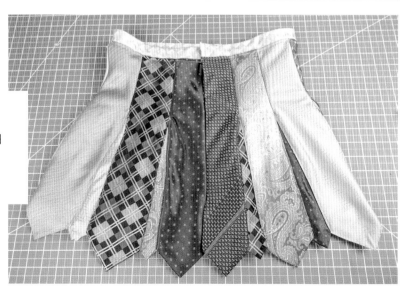

STEP 12

Prepare your zipper. I used an invisible zipper, which are generally 7 to 9 inches for a skirt. If you need to shorten your zipper, mark the desired length, sew (and back stitch) along your marking, and then cut ½ inch below your stitches. If you like, you can serge or zigzag stitch the raw edge to avoid fraying.

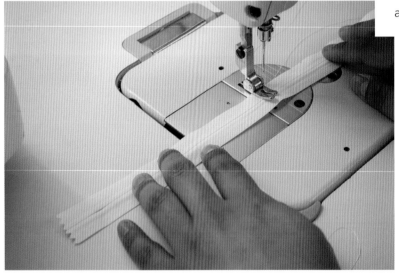

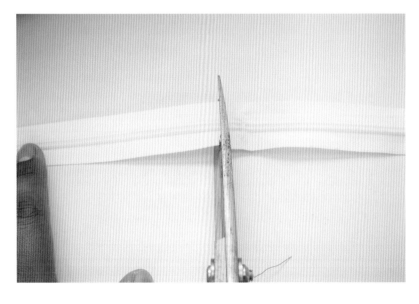

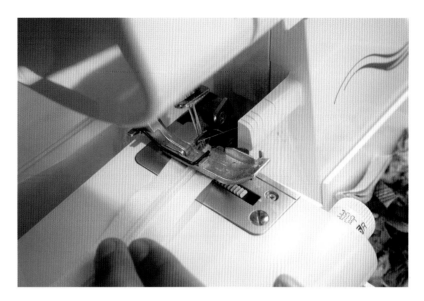

STEP 13

Flatten out the zipper teeth with an iron on both sides for easier sewing.

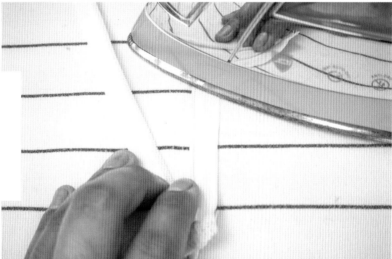

STEP 14

Insert your invisible zipper at the back of your skirt and sew in place. Use an invisible zipper foot, if you have one, for easier sewing.

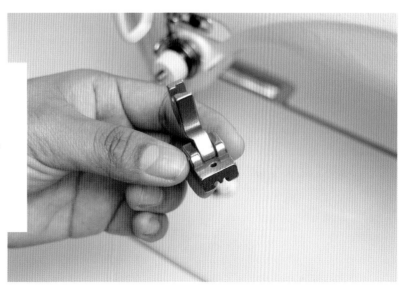

HOW TO SEW AN INVISIBLE ZIPPER

STEP 1

With the zipper all the way open, place it facedown along the edge of the lefthand back panel (right sides together). The zipper's teeth should be facing outwards, with the tape parallel to the seam. Check that the top of the zipper is flush with the top of the waistband, then clip, pin, or add a basting stitch to lightly secure it.

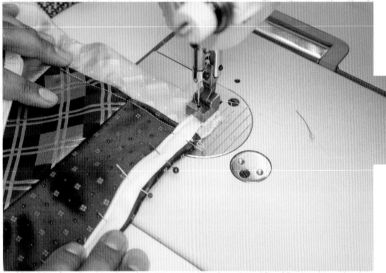

STEP 2

With your needle positioned up next to the zipper teeth, sew the zipper to your garment. Get as close as you can to the zipper pull, then backstitch at the end. If you have an invisible zipper foot, it will guide your zipper for you.

STEP 3

To sew the zipper to the other side, flip the zipper tape over once.

STEP 4

Flip the zipper tape again, so that the zipper teeth are also facing the right-hand side.

STEP 5

Clip, pin, or add a basting stitch to the zipper tape to hold it in position along the edge. Make sure it aligns along the top of the waist-band, too. Sew as you did in Step 2.

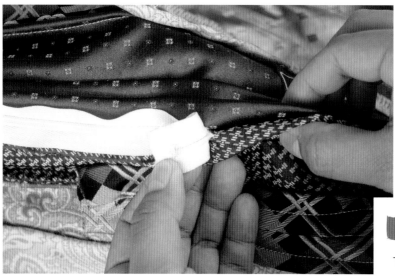

STEP 6

Turn the skirt inside out. Pin and sew the ties together below the zipper following along the zipper's stitch line. Sew all the way down.

STEP 7

If needed, add a hook and eye above your invisible zipper to secure.

FINAL LOOK

REMINDERS AND VARIATIONS

Iron down the zipper area so the zipper lays nicely in the seam. Put your iron at a low setting with minimal steam to avoid any fabric from melting in case there are synthetic fibers in the ties.

If your ties have a label sewn on it, you can seam rip it off so the label doesn't rub against your leg for extra comfortability.

PILLOWCASE TO TOTE BAG

Pillowcase

Scrap fabrics or linens

Fabric shears

Pins or clips

Grid ruler

Marking tool

Sewing machine or hand-sewing supplies

Optional: Serger or overlock machine

Estimated time: 2 hours

Skill Level: Intermediate

Tote bags are one of the most versatile accessories to have in your closet. On the way to the grocery store? Grab a tote bag! Heading to the coffee shop to do some work? Throw your items in a tote bag! Doing some shopping at the local flea market? Don't forget your tote bag! The best part about a tote bag is that you can find or customize one to fit your everyday needs. In this project, you'll upcycle a humble pillowcase and scrap fabrics into a do-it-all tote bag.

STEP 1

Lay your pillowcase flat, and mark 6 inches from the top and bottom on both long sides. For size reference, my pillowcase is large.

Your measurements may vary depending on the size of your pillowcase. Sew down the opening edge of your pillowcase to have one flat piece of fabric.

STEP 2

Draw a line to connect the two bottom marks, then do the same at the top.

STEP 3

Mark the middle of the pillow-case with a line going from top to bottom. You can find the middle by folding the pillow-case in half from the sides, and lightly marking it along the fold. Use a ruler to straighten out your lines.

STEP 4

Decide the length of your straps with a measuring tape, then double that measurement to determine the total length of material you need. I wanted 50-inch straps, one on each side, so I needed about 100 inches worth of material.

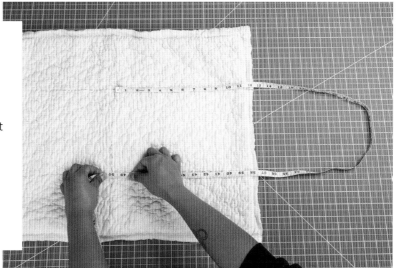

STEP 5

Fold your scrap fabric in half. From the fold mark and cut out a strap that is half of the length measured out in the previous step. Add in a 1-inch seam allowance.

For the width, mark up about 4 inches. Seam allowance is included in this measurement.

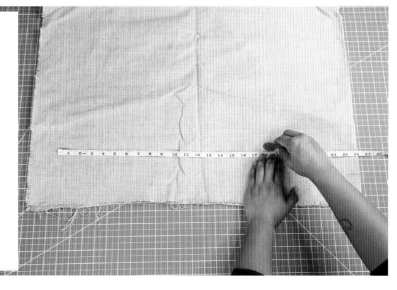

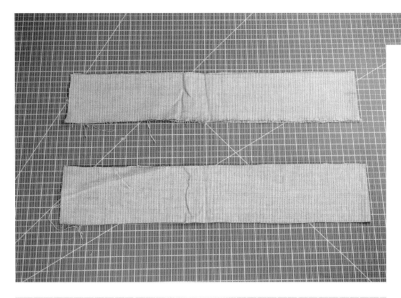

In my example, since one strap will be a total of 50 inches, I'll be marking a length of 26 inches on the fold (25-inch strap plus a 1-inch seam allowance) so that when it's opened up, it will equal to the length I need.

Cut out a second strap to match the length and width of your first strap. You can do this by placing it on the fold of the scrap fabric and cutting along it to match.

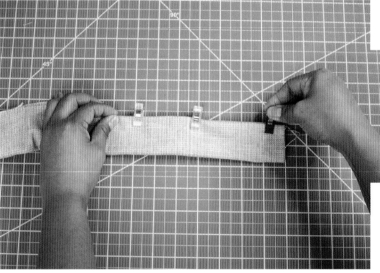

STEP 6

Hem each strap by folding in ½ inch along each long edge of the strap (wrong sides together) and sew along the edge to secure. Repeat for the second strap.

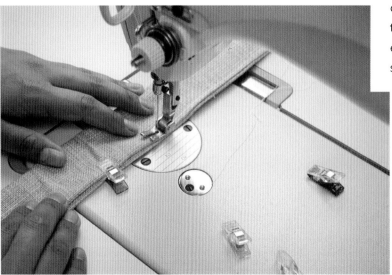

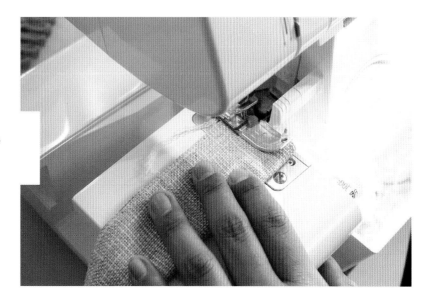

Serge or zigzag stitch at the raw ends.

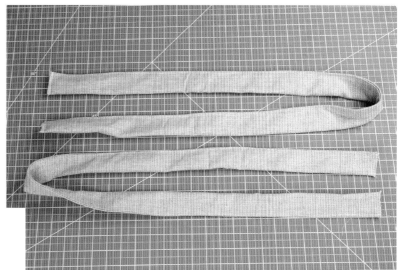

STEP 7

Pin or clip the two straps together by their ends to form one continuous loop. Sew the two seams.

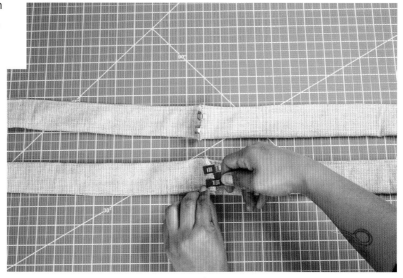

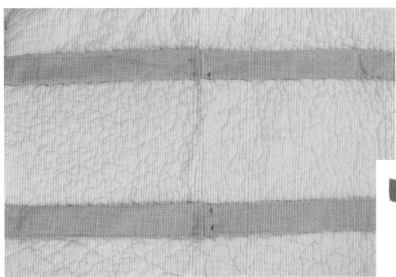

STEP 8

Pin the strap loop with its middle seams on the middle line on the pillowcase. Pin the inside edge of the top strap above and along the upper line on your pillowcase, then pin the lower strap's inside edge below and along the bottom line on the pillowcase.

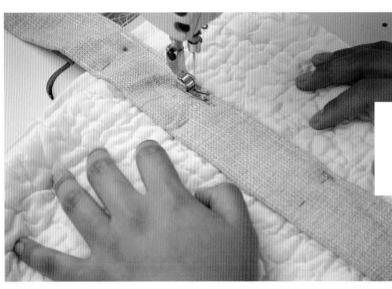

Sew along both edges to connect the straps firmly to the pillowcase.

STEP 9

Fold the pillowcase in half crosswise with right sides facing inward, then pin or clip along all four edges. Mark out a 2x2-inch square in each bottom corner of the tote bag.

Cut out the squares.

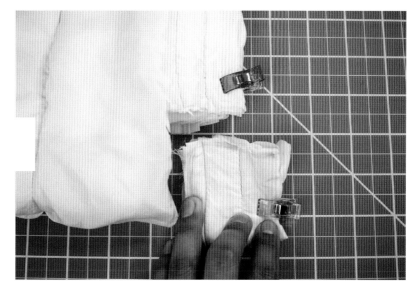

STEP 10

Sew along both sides of the tote bag, using a ½-inch seam allowance. Do not sew the notches you made.

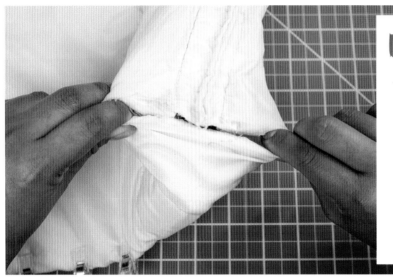

STEP 11

Grasp the front and back of the tote bag on either side of one notch's inner corner. Pull outward, so the bottom of the side seam meets the bottom of the tote bag (imagine you're stretching the corners of an open mouth to bring the lips together).

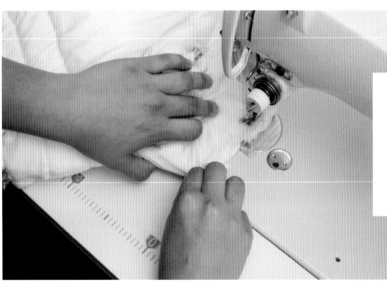

Pin and sew along the edge (closed lips). Repeat for the second notch.

Serge or zigzag stitch any raw edges.

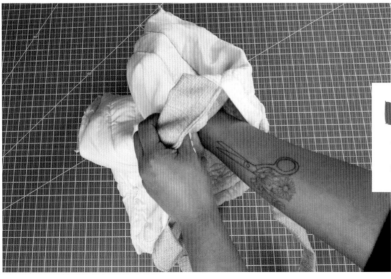

STEP 12

Turn your tote bag right-side out.

FINAL LOOK

REMINDERS AND VARIATIONS

To make a unique tote bag, let the fabric speak for you! Choose a pillowcase with character in its fabric. Customize the straps too. The example's measurements should enable the tote to fit on your shoulder comfortably. Adjust the strap length accordingly for a handheld tote bag.

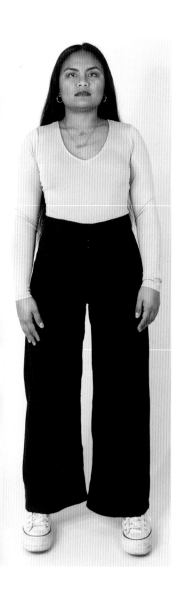

NO-SEW FABRIC WEAVING

WHAT YOU NEED

Long-sleeve top
Ruler
Marking tool
Fabric shears

Estimated time: 1 to 2 hours, depending on your design

Skill Level:: Easy

TIP:

When choosing your garment, make sure that it has enough stretch to it. The fabric will be a lot easier to weave through!

You don't always need to sew to complete a one-of-a-kind upcycling project! Woven (also known as braided) t-shirts have been around for decades and are a simple way to quickly spice up the plain look of a garment by adding texture and dimension.

In this project, you will learn how to create an intricately woven design using only a pair of scissors and your fingers. Apply this technique to a stretchy garment of choice for best results.

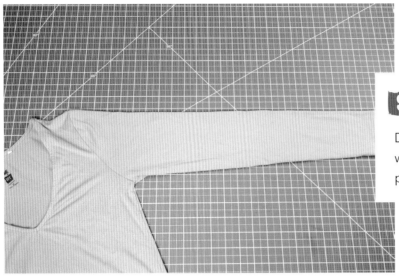

STEP 1

Decide where you want the weaving to be. For the example, I'll start with a sleeve edge.

Lay your shirt flat. Starting at the sleeve hem, cut a horizontal slit about 1 inch to 1-½ inches long on the edge. Move up about ½ inch to 1 inch and cut a second strip of the same length. Continue toward the shoulder, cutting strips of the same length and distance apart.

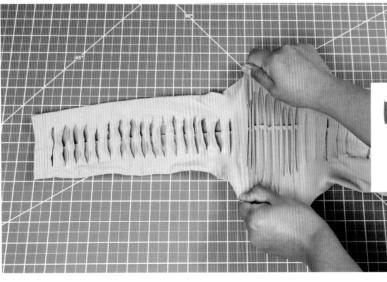

STEP 2

Lightly stretch out the fabric along the cuts.

STEP 3

To weave the strips, start from the top of your garment and work your way down to the hem.

Grab the first strip.

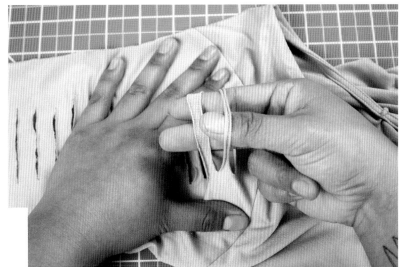

STEP 4

With your thumb and two fingers, reach underneath the first strip to grab the second one.

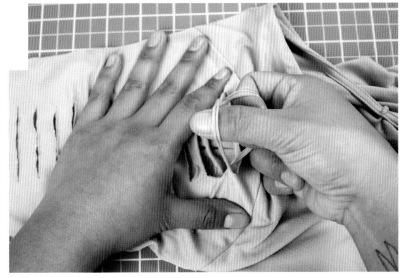

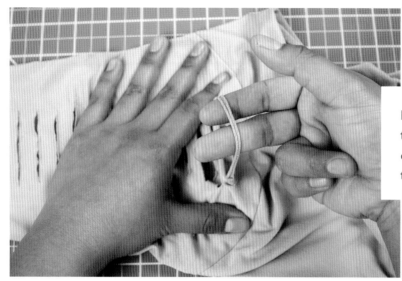

Pull the second strip under the first and up, so the second strip makes a loop above the first.

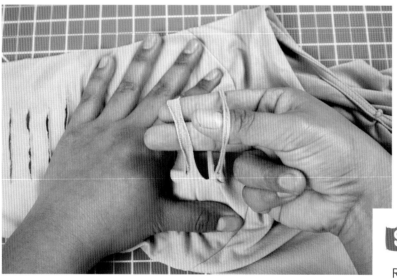

STEP 5

Reach through the second strip's loop, grab the third strip, and pull it up under the second to make another loop.

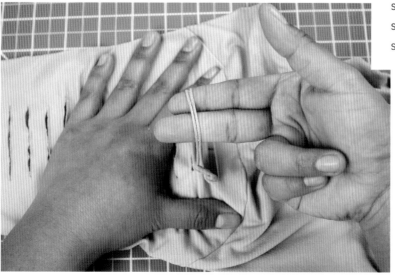

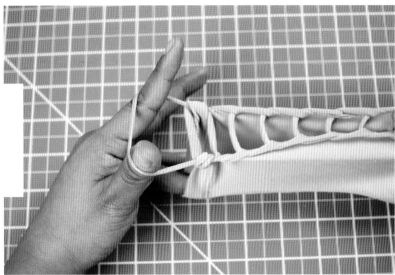

Keep reaching through the loop to pull up the strip below (repeating Steps 4 and 5) until you get to the last strip.

STEP 6

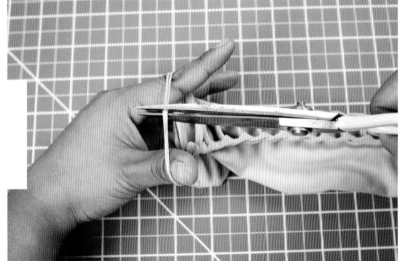

To prevent unraveling, cut the last strip through the middle.

Double knot each side to the previous strip's loop to secure the weave.

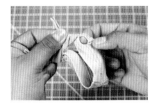   

STEP 7

To add additional weaving, mark style lines and fold along the line. Cut your strips along the fold (as for the sleeve) and repeat Steps 3 through 6.

FINAL LOOK

REMINDERS AND VARIATIONS

Once you've mastered this simple weaving method, experiment with different slit lengths, widths, and placements! However, keep the distances between your slits consistent. If your slits are too far apart, the strips will come out too wide. If you cut the slits too closely, the strips may rip apart in the middle.

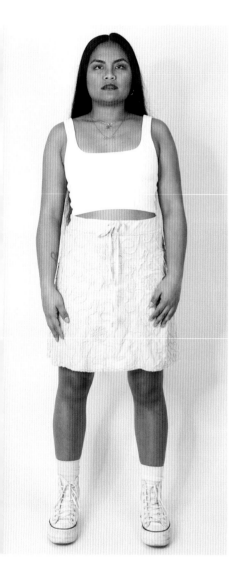  

DYEING A GARMENT

Garment of choice

Fabric dye

Stove (or any option to heat water)

Pot *(not used for cooking)* or
large bucket

Stirring utensil *(not used for cooking)*

Sink

Washing machine and dryer

Estimated time: 1 to 2 hours

Skill Level: Easy/Intermediate,
depending on garment chosen
for dyeing

After repeated washes, your favorite hot pink denim pants might lose their pigment over time. But that doesn't mean they're destined for the donations bag. You can use a bit of fabric dye to refresh them—or even change their color. Have you ever gone thrifting only to discover a near-perfect garment in a far-from-perfect color? In this project, you'll learn how to dye that secondhand find to change its color and give it new life in just a few short steps.

STEP 1

Heat a large pot of water. You'll need around 3 gallons of water per 1 pound of fabric being dyed.

BEST PRACTICES FOR DYEING

RIT dye is a common brand known for its selection of dyes and pigments in both boxed and liquid form. *Make sure that you choose the right type of dye for the fabric content of your garment.* There are specific dyes for polyester/man-made fibers.

The steps in this project demonstrate the basic procedure. Always follow the instructions on your chosen dye to prepare for dyeing.

Pour the hot water into the sink or a large bucket.

TIP:

Make sure to prewash your garment to get rid of any shrinkage, dirt, or stains.

STEP 2

Add about ¼ cup of salt to the water for cotton and linen fabrics to help the dye adhere better to the garment. For wool and silk, use white vinegar.

My skirt is 100% cotton.

Stir the salt or vinegar into the water thoroughly.

STEP 3

Add your dye into the water and stir. The amount of dye you use depends on the weight of your fabric and the color you want to achieve.

Test the color by dipping a paper towel or a swatch of your fabric.

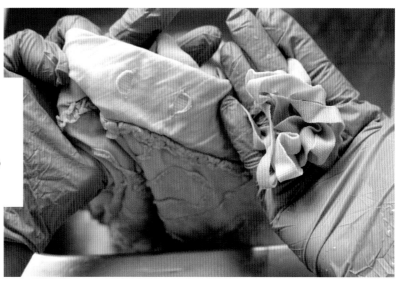

STEP 4

Before dyeing, remove any drawstrings on your garment so you can dye them separately.

Submerge your garment into the dye and stir your fabric occasionally. Leave for around 10 minutes or adjust the time accordingly to achieve the color you want. The longer you leave a garment in the dye, the more pigmented it will become.

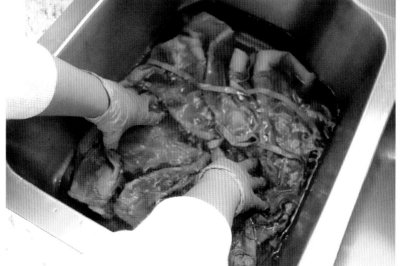

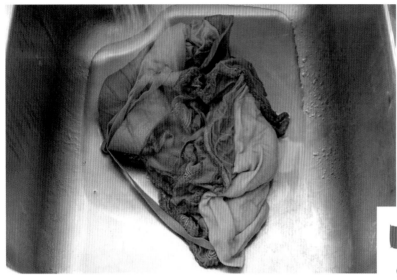

STEP 5

Once the desired time is up, put the dyed garment into cold water and rinse until the water runs clear.

STEP 6

Launder the garment, using mild detergent and a cold cycle. Hang to dry or use a dryer. Don't worry: A color change is normal once the garment is completely dry. If you want to achieve a darker shade, you can re-dye the garment using the same steps.

FINAL LOOK

REMINDERS AND VARIATIONS

With dyeing fabric, there are so many possibilities. Play around with different designs, dye specific sections, or create different effects! You could also try natural dyeing techniques with coffee, turmeric, fruit, flowers, and more.

Be aware that some garments may need more than one dye job, as pigment may wash off after laundering. You can also use Rit ColorStay Fixative after dyeing and before rinsing to help lock in the color.

SWEATER TO VEST

Sweater

Fabric shears

Seam ripper

Marking tool

Grid ruler

Pins or sewing clips

Sewing machine

Optional: Serger or overlock machine

Estimated time: 30 minutes to 1 hour

Skill Level: Easy

Do you have a favorite sweater that's been sitting in your closet for years, but you can't seem to get rid of it? Keep it in your rotation by turning it into a sweater vest! Vests are the perfect, year-round layering piece that can go over t-shirts, long sleeves, or button-ups.

In this project, I'll show you how to transform a sweater into a vest. You'll learn to carefully seam rip sections of a garment and keep the original bottom hem intact to create a new cropped look.

STEP 1

Lay your sweater flat and cut or seam rip the sleeves off.

You can serge or zigzag stitch any raw edges, if you like.

CHOOSING A SWEATER

Be mindful of the sweater material that you choose. Some fabrics may be more delicate than others. Closely knit sweaters tend to be easier to sew over than loosely knit ones.

STEP 2

With the right side of fabric out, fold over and pin a ½-inch seam allowance at the armholes.

Sew using a zigzag or stretch stitch to hem the armholes.

TIP:

On fabrics with stretch, it is better to sew with a zigzag or stretch-stitch setting to minimize thread breakage. Sewing with a straight stitch has a risk of the hem or seams ripping apart.

You can stop here with your completed sweater vest or continue on if you'd like to change the length of your vest.

STEP 3

Determine the length you want your vest to be and mark the new hem line, if needed. Fold the bottom of the vest over, right sides together, to the desired length.

STEP 4

Pin along the seam of the ribbing where it joins the sweater body or clip along the hem fold.

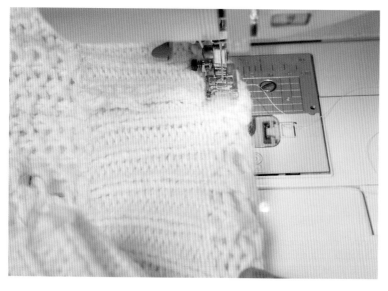

STEP 5

Sew along the ribbing's seam, joining the layers together. With this method, you're able to keep the original ribbing and hem without cutting and reattaching it.

Cut off the excess fabric while leaving a small seam allowance, serge or zigzag stitch the raw edges, then fold the ribbing back down—done!

FINAL LOOK

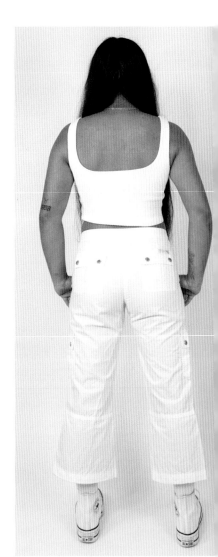

PANTS TO SKIRT

Pants

Fabric shears

Seam ripper

Pins or clips

Grid ruler

Marking tool

Sewing machine or hand-sewing supplies

Optional: Serger or overlock machine, rotary cutter

Estimated time: 1 to 2 hours

Skill Level: Easy

TIP:

Choose pants that fit you nicely at the waist for minimal alterations.

Upcycling can be challenging, but that's what makes the process fun! The best projects consist of transforming an item into a brand-new design that doesn't look like what it was initially. One garment has the potential to turn into many different designs. I've seen people turn thrifted belts into tops, empty rice sacks into jackets, and comforters into dresses. To push yourself creatively, it's important to start with a basic project that will act as a foundation for any future designs you have in mind.

In this project, you'll learn how to take apart a pair of pants at its seams and turn it into a skirt! This can be done with any pants style and fabric, so choose a fun pair to transform.

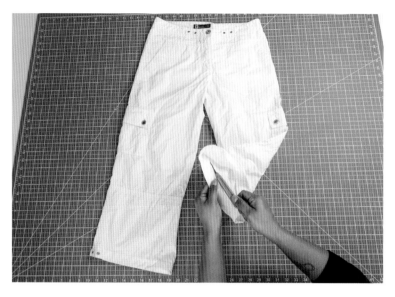

STEP 1

Lay your pants flat and determine the length of your skirt. For a shorter skirt, measure up from the pant legs' hems, mark each leg (remember to allow for the hem), and cut straight along the guideline if needed.

To make your skirt an inch or two longer than the pants, like I did, seam rip each leg's bottom hem to release.

STEP 2

Use your seam ripper to open up the inseam on each leg.

STEP 3

On the front, mark 1 to 2 inches below the zipper fly. Seam rip the crotch line up to your mark.

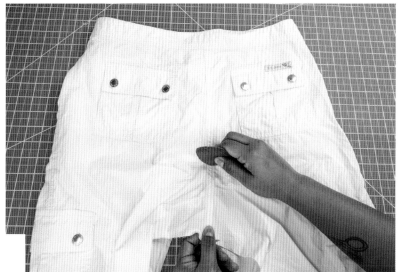

Flip the pants over and seam rip up to within a few inches of the bottom of the back rise.

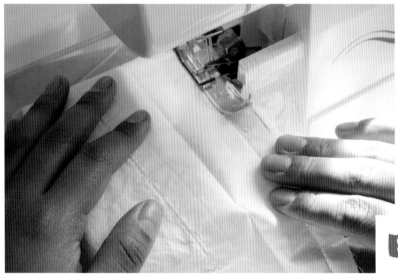

STEP 4

Serge or zigzag stitch any raw edges. Use an iron to straighten out any opened seams.

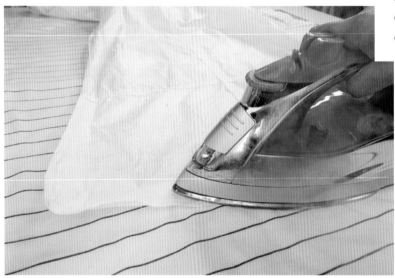

STEP 5

Below the front fly, fold the overlapping piece underneath itself (like tucking in an envelope flap). You want the flap hidden and the fold to seamlessly match up in a straight line with the pants inseam. Pin to secure it before continuing.

STEP 6

Continue folding the right leg's edge inward (like a hem), pinning it over the left leg's raw front edge as you go. Sew the new center seam from the crotch to the hem.

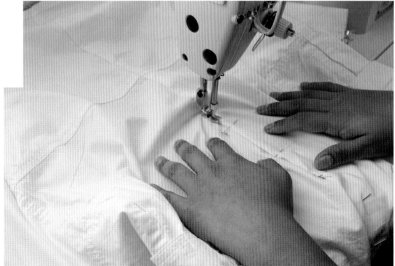

STEP 7

On the back side, lay the back-rise piece flat so the halves overlap. Pin it in place, following along the upper edge until it ends.

Fold the inseam edge under to create a hem and pin. Repeat along the edge of the opposite leg's inseam. The opening this creates in the back ensures that the skirt won't restrict your legs when you move around.

Sew along the back-rise edge and inseams to connect and then hem the pieces.

STEP 8

Cut off any hanging excess fabric on the inside of the pants, and serge or zigzag stitch any raw edges.

STEP 9

If needed, hem the bottom of the skirt to your desired length.

FINAL LOOK

REMINDERS AND VARIATIONS

This classic pants-to-skirt transformation also works on shorts and trousers. Keep in mind, though, that the baggier the pant leg, the more fabric you'll have to make a spacious skirt.

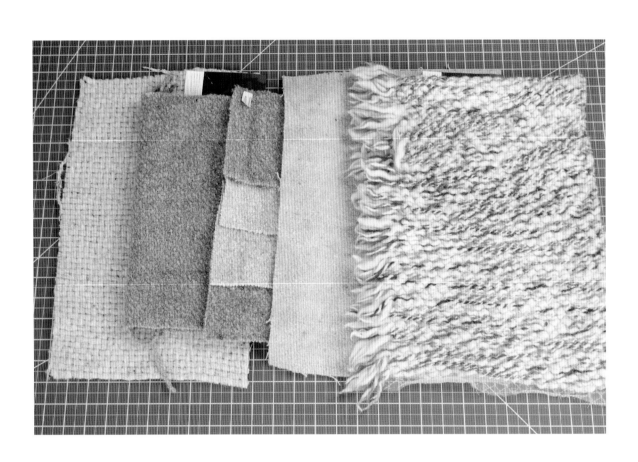

FABRIC SCRAPS TO PATCHWORK SCARF

WHAT YOU NEED

Scrap fabric

Fabric shears

Pins or clips

Sewing machine or hand-sewing supplies

Grid ruler

Marking tool

Optional: Serger or overlock machine, favorite scarf for size reference

Estimated time: 1 to 2 hours

Skill Level: Easy

TIP:

Choose your fabrics wisely. Keep in mind the comfortability of the lining, as you don't want it to irritate your neck during all day wear. Sherpa is a great choice that will be soft to the touch and keep you warm at the same time. Satin or silk linings are also a great pick for a lightweight feel, especially for warm weather.

Scarves are a versatile accessory to have on hand in your closet, no matter what the season! Put on a wool scarf to keep warm during a chilly day, or go for a thinner, skinnier scarf during the summer months. You could even style a scarf as a top or wrap it around as a skirt!

In this project, you'll put your patchwork skills to work again upcycling scrap fabrics into a lined scarf.

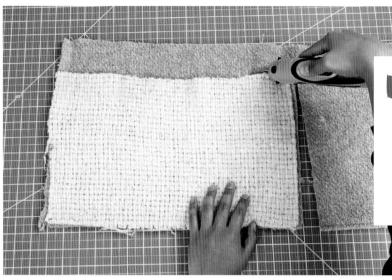

STEP 1

Decide the length of your scarf. Cut your fabric scraps to the size you want, factoring in a ½-inch seam allowance all the way around.

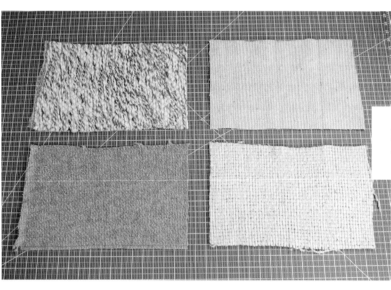

I cut four fabric scraps into 15x10-inch rectangles.

STEP 2

Pin and sew all your pieces together to create one length.

STEP 3

Place the patchwork on top of your chosen lining fabric. Cut out a piece to match the length and width of your patchwork fabric.

STEP 4

Pin the main fabric and lining right sides together.

STEP 5

Sew all the way around, leaving one bottom seam open.

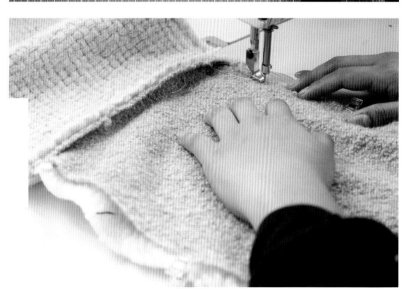

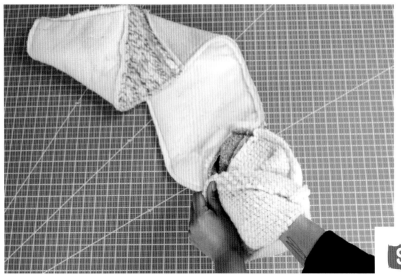

STEP 6

Reach through your scarf and turn it right side out.

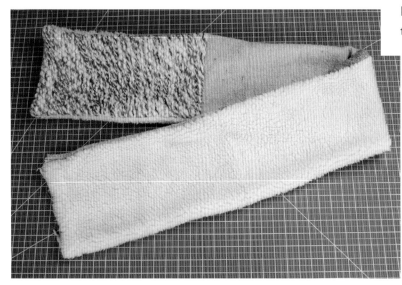

STEP 7

Fold the bottom edges inward all the way around, pin, and sew to close the opening.

FINAL LOOK

REMINDERS AND VARIATIONS

Add character to your scarf by combining different textures and prints, but make sure they match in weight so that one side doesn't stretch more than the other during wear.

KNIT SWEATER TO SHRUG AND TUBE TOP

Sweater

Pins or clips

Grid ruler

French curve ruler

Marking tool

Sewing machine or hand-sewing supplies

Optional: Serger or overlock machine

Estimated time: 1 hour

Skill Level: Easy

TIP:

Choose a sweater that fits you well for minimal alterations! Rib knit sweaters work best for this project.

Some upcycling projects may yield leftover fabric, and that's okay. Instead of setting it aside, try to think of other ways you could use those extra pieces. For example, if you cut off the sleeves from a sweater, you could easily repurpose them to be leg warmers. If you turn a pair of pants into shorts, cut open those scrap pant legs and turn them into a tote bag. There's a project for everything, so take a moment to examine your scraps and get creative!

In this project, I'll show you how to create two upcycled pieces out of one garment so that nothing goes to waste. You can wear the pieces together for an effortless look or separately for different occasions.

STEP 1

Determine how long you'd like your shrug, usually a few inches below the armholes. Measure and mark corresponding points below each.

Using the French curve, connect both marks with a slightly curved line.

STEP 2

Cut, following along the curve while leaving about a ½-inch seam allowance.

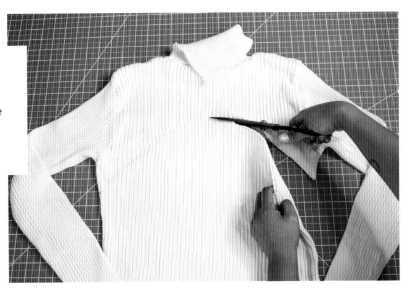

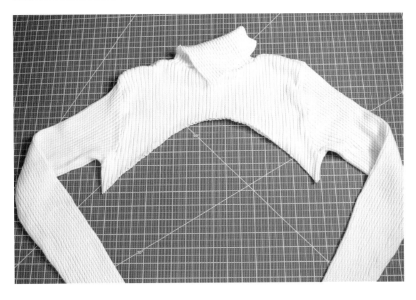

Serge or zigzag stitch the raw edges to avoid any fraying. This will be the shrug.

STEP 3

Fold to the wrong side, pin, and hem all around your shrug piece.

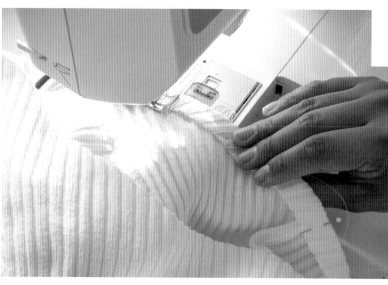

STEP 4

With the rest of the sweater's fabric, determine the tube-top silhouette you want to create. You can cut the piece to your desired tube-top shape like a rectangle, or cut along the bottom to create a curved hem.

TIP:

Try on your garment throughout the sewing process to test the fit and make sure you like it, especially if you're working with a stretch fabric. Stretch fabric may tend to lose its stretch over time with wear.

For any fit adjustments, take in the sides of the tube top: Mark an equal distance from each side seam.

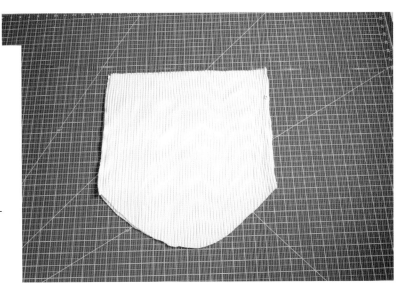

Cut off any excess fabric, leaving a seam allowance, then sew the new side seam.

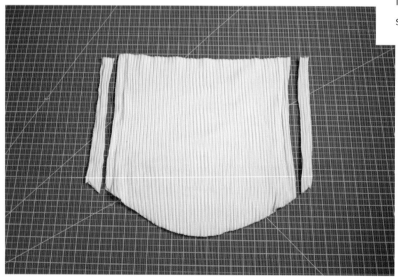

FINAL LOOK

REMINDERS AND VARIATIONS

This project also works on plain sweatshirts and long-sleeved t-shirts!

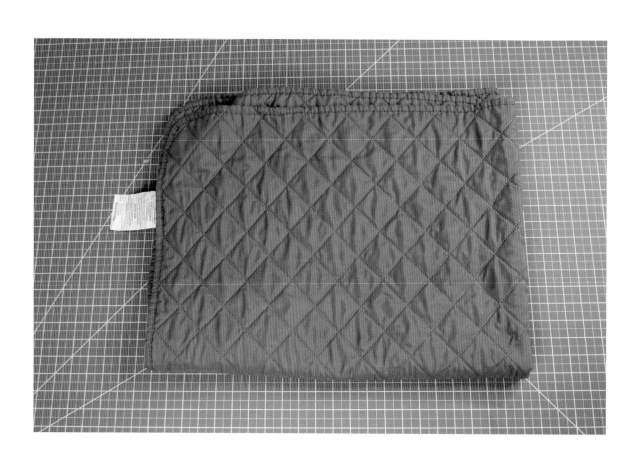

BLANKET TO TRIANGLE BAG

Blanket

Scrap fabrics or linens

Fabric scissors

Pins or clips

Grid ruler

Marking tool

Sewing machine or hand-sewing supplies

Optional: Serger or overlock machine

Estimated time: 1 to 2 hours

Skill Level: Easy

Certain bags pair well with specific outfits. A sparkly clutch may match perfectly with an evening gown, or a nylon cross-body bag with a casual athleisure outfit. You might even feel the need to switch up your everyday tote bag from time to time. Instead of going for a basic square tote, how about a triangle for a change? In this project, I'll show you how to cut and fold a blanket to create a distinctive triangle bag.

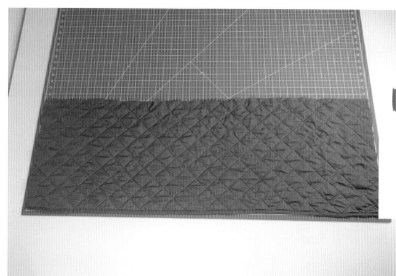

STEP 1

To make a medium-size bag, measure out and cut a 15x60-inch rectangle from your blanket.

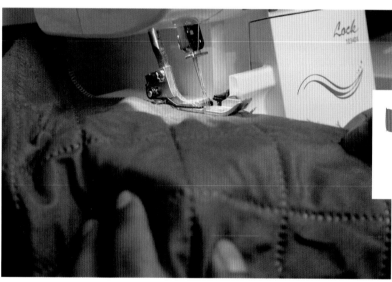

STEP 2

Serge or zigzag stitch any raw edges.

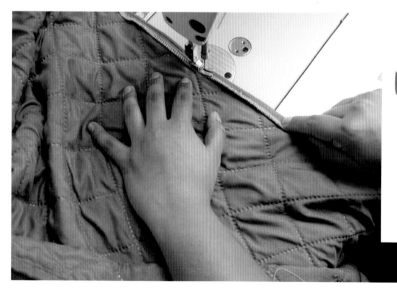

STEP 3

Fold over ½ inch along each edge, pin, and sew on the right side to create a hem all the way around the fabric. Pin and sew the hems one side at a time, if that's easier for you.

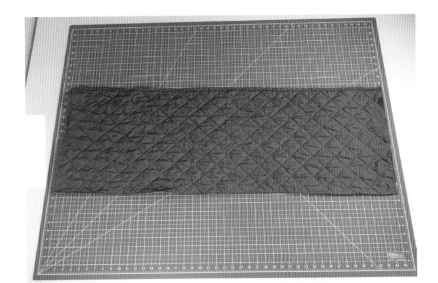

Lay your fabric flat with the right side up.

STEP 4

Fold the top-left corner diagonally toward the bottom (right sides together).

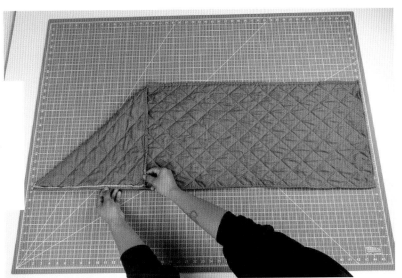

STEP 5

Fold the bottom-right corner diagonally toward the top (right sides together).

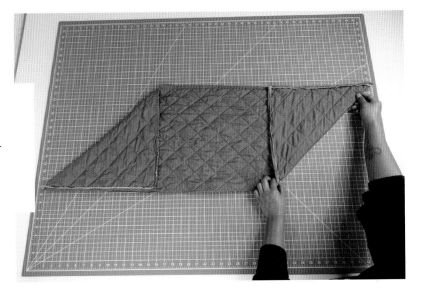

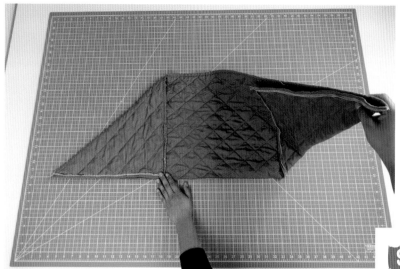

STEP 6

Fold the right side diagonally, toward the middle.

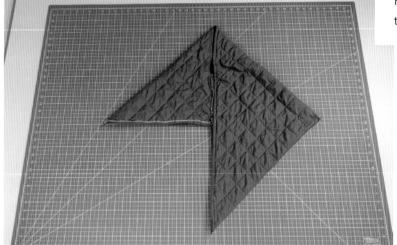

STEP 7

Pin or clip along the touching edges on the front of the bag, then sew, flip it over and do the same on the back. Sew the seams using a ½-inch seam allowance.

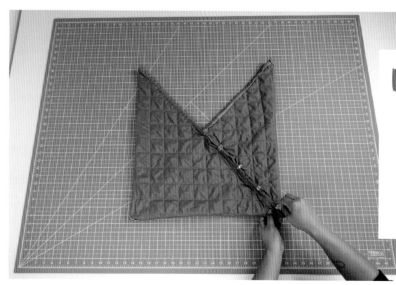

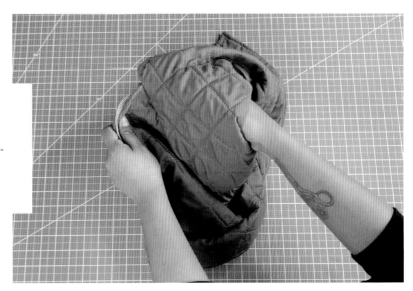

STEP 8

Turn your bag inside out (hiding the seams from Step 7 to the inside).

STEP 9

From your scrap fabric, cut out a strip that is 8 inches long and 2-½ inches wide.

You can serge or zigzag stitch both lengthwise raw edges. Make a ¼-inch hem along the widths.

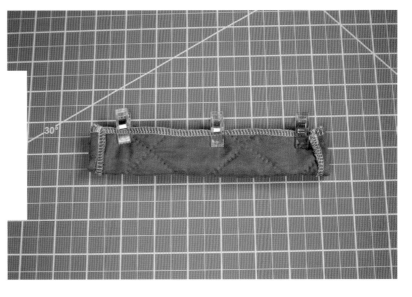

STEP 10

Fold your strip in half lengthwise and right sides together. Sew a ¼-inch seam along that edge.

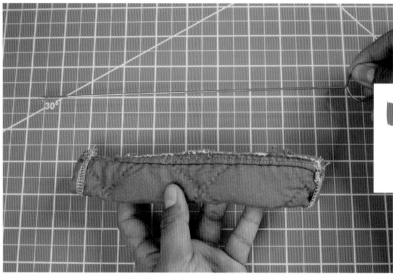

STEP 11

Using a loop turner, turn the tube of fabric inside out.

STEP 12

Grab the top-left corner of your tote bag, and pull it through the tube using a loop turner.

How to Use a Loop Turner

STEP 1

Put the tool through the fabric
you wish to turn inside out.

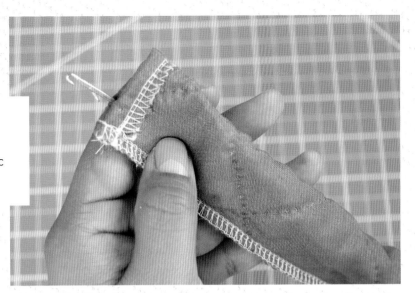

STEP 2

Connect the tool's latch hook
to the fabric of one corner.

STEP 3

Pull the loop turner and guide the fabric with your hands
until the fabric is completely turned back around. You'll end
up with a piece of fabric that looks like a tube.

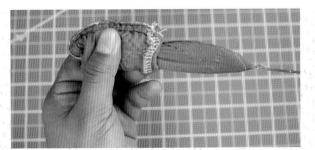

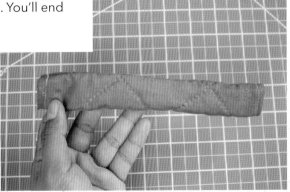

STEP 13

Slightly overlap the left cover on top of the right corner, then pin and sew.

STEP 14

Pull the tube over the corners that you sewed together to cover the join.

FINAL LOOK

REMINDERS AND VARIATIONS

When customizing the size of your bag, make a sample bag out of scrap fabric to make sure your measurements line up nicely.

FABRIC SCRAPS TO RUFFLED GLOVES

Scrap fabric or garment large
enough to fit your hand and up
your arm

Fabric shears

Tailor's chalk or water-soluble marker

Pins

Optional: Grid ruler

Estimated time: 30 minutes to
1 hour

Skill Level: Easy

TIP:

This project works best with
a fabric that contains stretch
for comfort and ease. Test out
your fabric first to make sure
it goes around your fingers
and arms.

Gloves are a great way to add a statement to a fun, eclectic
outfit or to serve a function by protecting your fingers and
keeping warm throughout the day. With different sizes to
choose from, ranging from wrist to shoulder length, experiment with styling to create your gloves for any occasion. Put
on fun rings and bracelets for an accessory overload or pair
gloves with short-sleeved shirts to add additional color and
texture along your arms.

In this project, you'll customize a pair of gloves to fit you.
Make your gloves in sleek, stretchy leather, or go for sparkly
lace and a classy, elevated feel.

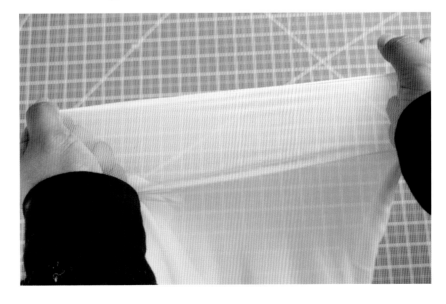

STEP 1

Fold your fabric in half, right sides together, and pin it so that it doesn't move.

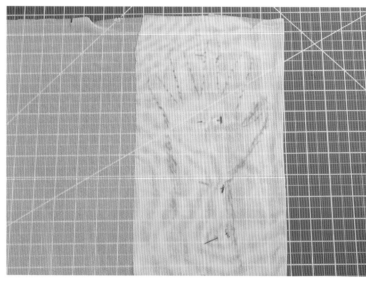

STEP 2

Trace around your hand and along your arm to your desired length. Make sure to spread your fingers when tracing around your hand!

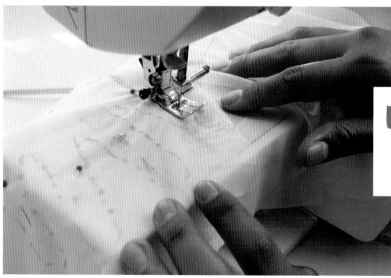

STEP 3

Stitch along your markings using a zigzag or stretch stitch.

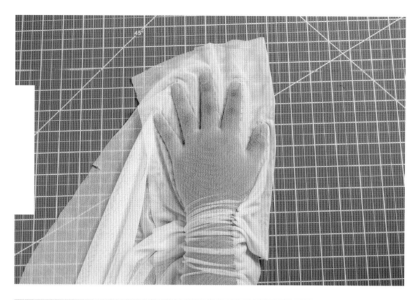

STEP 4

Remove the pins and try on the glove to check the fit. Adjust and stitch as needed.

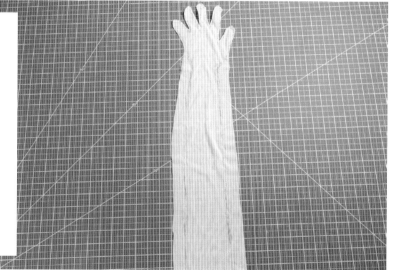

Carefully cut any excess fabric off. At the fingers and along the palms, cut as close as you can to the stitch line, but not through it.

At the wrist and along the arm, cut off the excess fabric, leaving around a 1- to 2-inch seam allowance. This creates the ruffles.

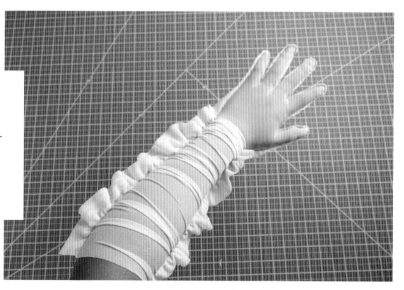

STEP 5

Try on the glove. Cut off any excess fabric or adjust the ruffles as needed. Repeat the steps to make the opposite glove.

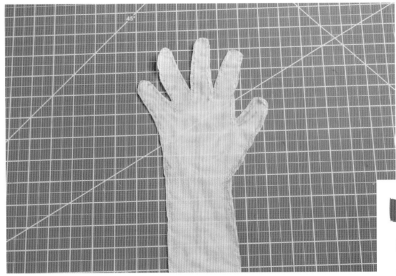

STEP 6

(Optional)

Don't want the ruffle effect? Cut around your glove as close as you can get to the stitch line, leaving about a ⅛-inch seam allowance.

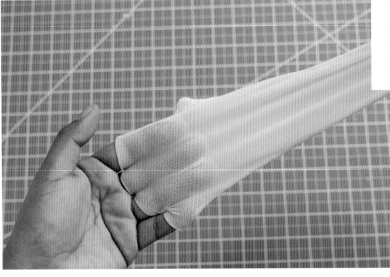

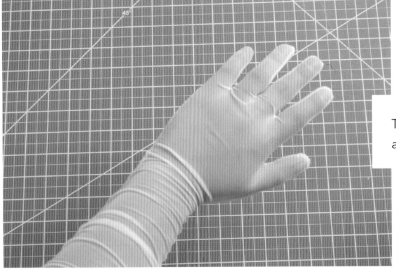

Turn your glove inside out for a clean look.

FINAL LOOK

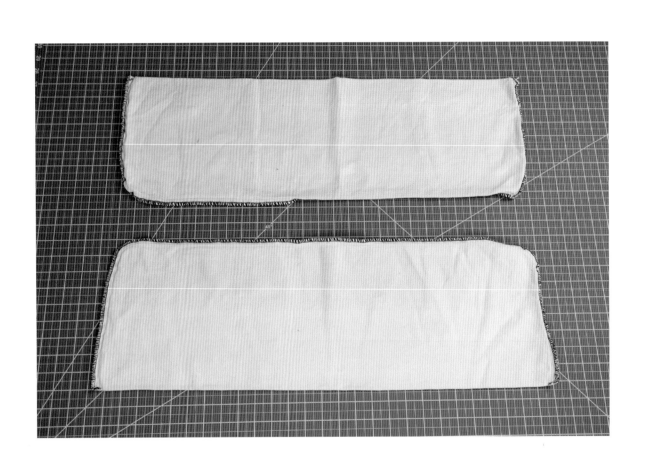

FABRIC SCRAPS TO BOOT COVERS

WHAT YOU NEED

Boots (calf or knee high rather than ankle height)

Fabric

Fabric shears

Paper scissors

Pins or clips

Grid ruler

Pattern-making or kraft paper

Marking tools

Sewing machine or hand-sewing supplies

Optional: Serger or overlock machine, French curve ruler

Estimated time: 1 to 2 hours

Skill Level: Easy

Versatile, interchangeable, and customizable designs are the future of fashion. The design detail on a garment can be as simple as a drawstring to change the length of a skirt or as complex as zippers that convert a jacket to a vest. By incorporating clothing and accessories that can be worn multiple ways into your closet, you'll be able to get more use out of the pieces. Plus, it's a great way to play around with styling!

Do you have a pair of favorite boots that you wish you had in multiple colors? Instead of buying brand new, save your money! In this project, I'll show you how to spice up a pair of boots by adding a removable cover. You'll learn how to create a pattern to fit your boots, then sew custom fabric covers to go onto them.

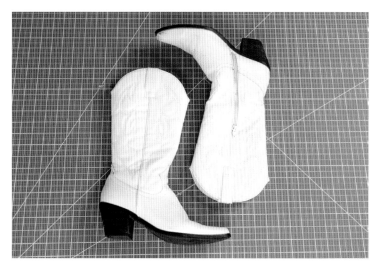

STEP 1

Lay a boot on top of the pattern paper. Trace around the shaft and calf area.

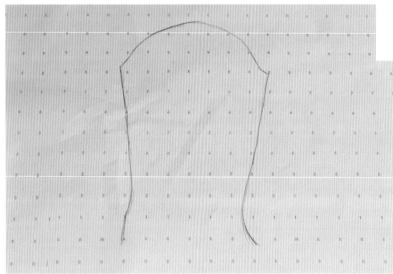

CHOOSING YOUR BOOT FABRIC

If you want a structured look for your boot cover, opt for a thicker, mid- to heavy-weight fabric such as denim, canvas, or leather as opposed to a lightweight woven cotton.

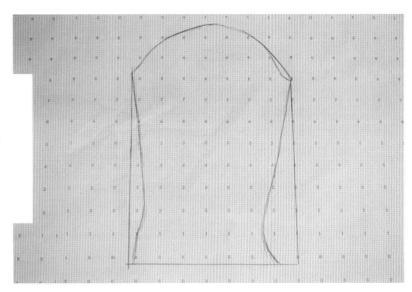

STEP 2

Straighten out your lines and fix any curves. Connect your lines at the bottom and remove the stray markings.

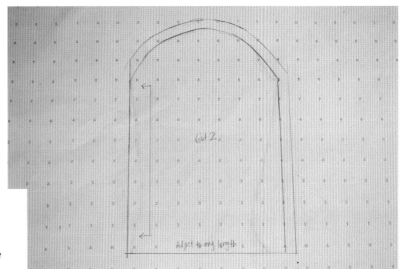

STEP 3

Add a ½-inch seam allowance along the top and side. You can adjust the bottom length, depending on the style you want to go for. Cut out the pattern.

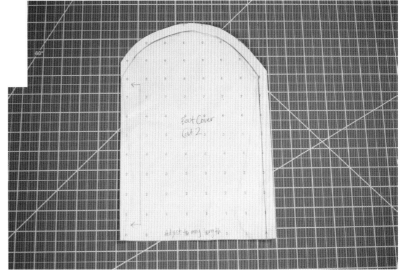

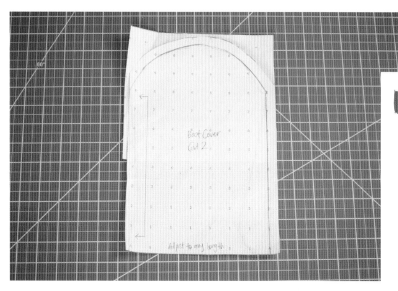

STEP 4

Make the pattern for the inner lining, which will help hold the boot covers on: Place the main pattern on top of another paper, trace around it, transfer all your markings, and cut out the lining pattern. It needs to be only ⅓ the height of the main pattern.

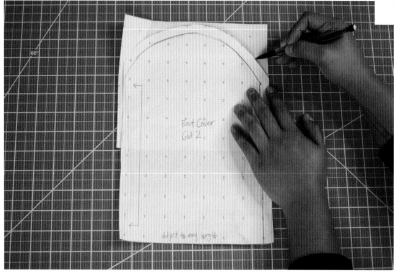

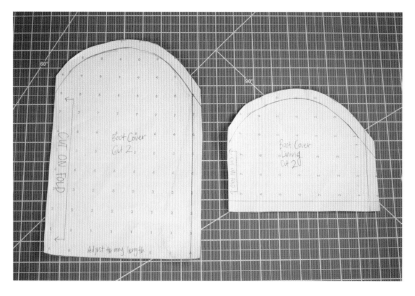

STEP 5

Fold your fabric lengthwise, place one side of each pattern along the fold, and cut out your fabric pieces.

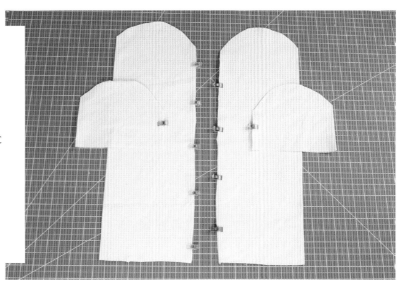

You need two of each pattern, one for each boot.

TIP:

To give your boot covers a stacked fabric look, cut fabric at least double the length of your main pattern: Fold your fabric horizontally as well as vertically and place your pattern so its bottom corner sits along both folds, then cut.

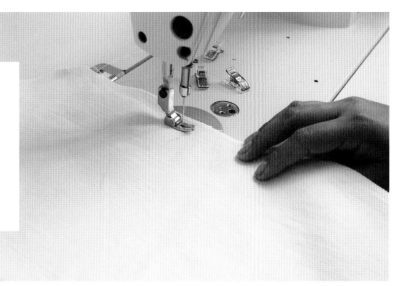

STEP 6

Pin and sew the side seams of both the covers and the linings. Serge or zigzag stitch the raw edges to avoid any fraying.

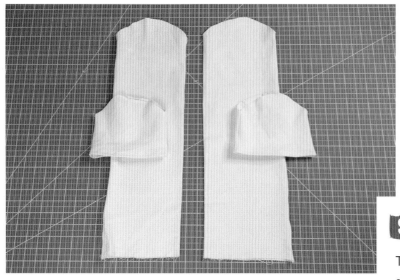

STEP 7

Turn the lining inside out, then slide it over the top of your main fabric, so both sets of right sides face each other and the tops line up.

Pin or clip along the top edges and sew.

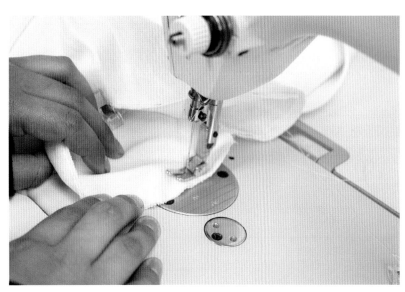

STEP 8

Before turning in the lining, clip along the top seam allowance, cutting almost to, but not through the stitches. These notches will help the curve lie flat.

STEP 9

Flip the lining to the inside of the boot covers. Hem the bottoms of the boot covers or leave them frayed.

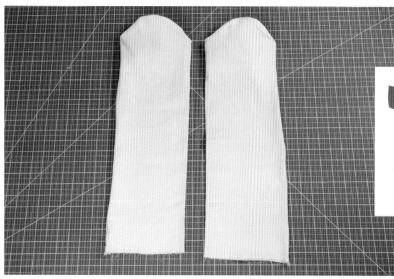

STEP 10

Slip the cover over your boot, sandwiching the boot top between the top fabric and lining.

FINAL LOOK

PANTS TO WAIST BAG

Pants

Fabric shears

Marking tool

Pins or clips

Sewing machine or hand-sewing tools

Optional: Serger or overlock machine

Estimated time: 30 minutes to 1 hour

Skill Level: Easy

Looking for a chic and modern alternative to a regular zippered fanny pack? Create an upcycled waist bag from a pair of pants! Just like a fanny pack, you can wear it around your waist or hips to hold your phone or anything else you need handy. It's a unique accessory full of character while also serving a function. In this project, I'll show you how to use the pant pockets and waistband, adding a new twist to their original form.

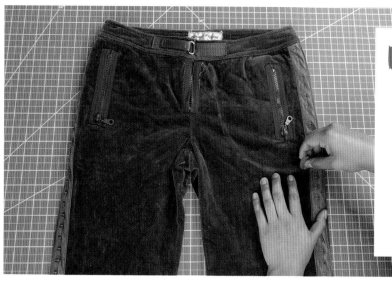

STEP 1

Lay your pants flat. Mark the shape of your bag: Start from the top of your zipper fly, and curve along the pocket to the side seam. Make sure to draw your bag outline large enough to capture the back pocket too, if your pants have one.

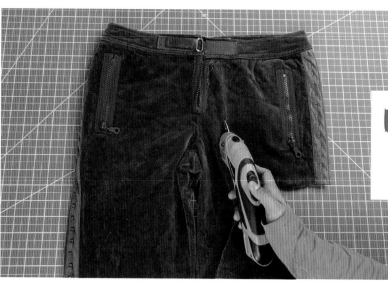

STEP 2

Cut through both layers of the pants following your marking.

STEP 3

Seam rip the waistband from the pants (but not from your bag). Remove the remaining pants.

STEP 4

Lay the bag body flat, and seam rip 1 inch or so along the waistband at each end.

Serge or zigzag stitch the raw edges.

Fold in and pin a ½-inch hem all the way around the bag and sew on the right side.

Resew the waistband onto the bag.

FINAL LOOK

UPCYCLING TIPS AND TRICKS

QUICK AND SIMPLE WAYS TO EMBELLISH

Here are five simple embellishments you need to know.

SEW ON APPLIQUE OR IRON-ON PATCHES

Applique and iron-on patches are a fun way to customize clothing with minimal effort!

WEAVE EMBROIDERY FLOSS OR YARN THROUGH KNITWEAR

Use a needle with a large eye or hand weave your yarn through a sweater to add a pop of color! See an example of this in the Knit Sweater Sweatshirt Duo project.

SEW TRIM TO SLEEVE AND PANT HEMS

Go to the trimmings section at your local fabric or craft store for inspiration, and then experiment with adding lace, ruffles, feathers, or whatever speaks to you to your hems. The choices are endless!

ADD UNIQUE STUDS OR SEQUINS

Buy a pack of studs or sequins that complement your project. Depending on what you choose, you can apply it with prongs or by hand sewing.

EMBROIDER SIMPLE ACCENTS

Add a simple design touch by embroidering hearts, stars, and flowers.

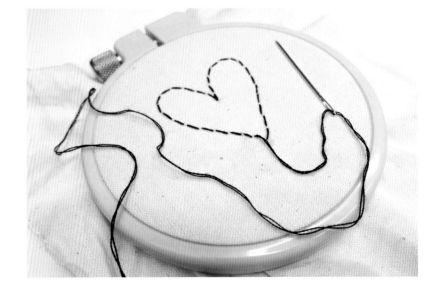

HOW TO CREATE A ONE-OF-A-KIND DESIGN

If you want to practice and elevate your design skills, follow these tips.

CONSIDER WHERE YOU'LL WEAR THE DESIGN

Do you want to create a design that is timeless or worn for a certain occasion? When will you wear this design: to attend a fancy dinner or run errands? Your answers will help you determine how comfortable you want your design to be and to decide on the elements you want to include. For an outfit headed to a fancy dinner, you might opt for an elegant fabric such as lace or satin for example. If you'll wear it while running errands, maybe you'll want to incorporate several pockets into your design.

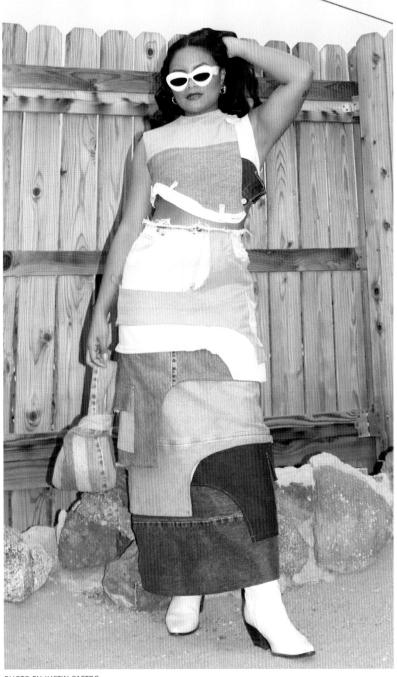

PHOTO BY JUSTIN CASTRO

PHOTOS BY MIKAEL-ANGELO TE & VANESSA MAE LIM

DECONSTRUCT THE GARMENT AND BRAINSTORM

To see the full potential of a garment you want to upcycle, take each of its details apart and lay everything in front of you. By removing every hem and seam, you'll be able to see exactly what you'll be working with. Take note of elements you want to keep. For example, on a pair of pants, you might want to include the belt loops into your final design or use the zipper in some way.

CHOOSE UNIQUE FABRICS OR MAKE YOUR OWN

Look for fabrics with a unique pattern, finish, or texture to add character into your design. Cut and piece together scraps for a patchwork look in a chosen color scheme or try a fabric manipulation technique, such as smocking. Your choices can make all the difference in making a design stand out.

INCLUDE FUNCTIONALITY IN YOUR GARMENT

Play around with garment closure options, such as adding a zipper, a lace-up detail, or snaps. Add D rings, O rings, or similar hardware to hang items on with a clasp. Make your design adjustable and convertible with a drawstring, elastic, buckles, or buttons.

ADD YOUR OWN TWIST TO A CURRENT FASHION TREND

If you like a current fashion trend but want to stand out, think of how you can incorporate that trend in a different way. If you love pleated skirts and want to create your own, for example, play around with a curved hemline instead of a straight hem. If you like patchwork t-shirts, cut the squares in a variety of sizes instead of making them uniform.

HOW TO MAKE CLEANER PROJECTS

As you continue to grow in your upcycling journey, you'll become more confident in your sewing skills. You may even consider selling your own upcycled designs. To add a bit of polish to your garments and banish that "homemade look," follow these tips.

PHOTO BY JUSTIN CASTRO

WASH AND DRY YOUR FABRICS BEFORE SEWING

Don't make the mistake of creating a garment only to have it shrink in the wash after one wear. Pre-wash your fabric to remove any dirt, chemicals, or excess dyes. Doing so also enables you to see how your fabric functions or changes after a wash.

USE THE RIGHT NEEDLE FOR THE FABRIC

To avoid any pulls or runs in your fabric, choose a needle that smoothly sews through it. As a general rule, the thinner and more delicate the fabric, the smaller the needle should be. If you're working with leather, layers of denim, or similarly thick fabrics, choose a heavy-duty needle. If you use a large needle on thin fabric, however, you may create unwanted holes.

CREATE A SAMPLE OF YOUR DESIGN BEFORE CUTTING INTO YOUR MAIN FABRIC

If it's your first time executing a specific design and you're unsure how it will turn out, try testing it on an extra garment or fabric that's similar to what you plan to work with. The risky part of upcycling is possibly not having any extra fabric left over in case you mess up, so there's nothing wrong with being extra sure of what you want to create.

SERGE OR ZIGZAG STITCH FABRIC EDGES TO PREVENT FRAYING

A well-made garment is nicely finished on the inside and out. If you're working with a fabric that tends to easily fray (woven fabrics like denim and cotton linen are notorious for this), factor in time to serge or zigzag stitch those edges. Even if a fabric looks like it won't fray, as you wear and wash the garment, it may start to fall apart over time.

PHOTO BY JEFF BONSOL

Snip off loose threads as you're sewing

Make it a habit to snip off those pesky thread tails as you work instead of trimming them all at once at the end. You're less likely to miss one this way, plus it will prevent threads from getting caught in the seams as you sew.

Continuously iron as you go

Throughout the steps of a project, have an iron hot and ready to remove any wrinkles in your fabric. Press open the seams you create, and go over hems to lock in those stitches.

PHOTO BY ASHLEY CHANG

RESOURCES

Check out these additional creators, books, and online resources that have guided and inspired me throughout my fashion journey over the years.

Books

9 Heads by Nancy Riegelman

Draping for Apparel Design by Helen Joseph-Armstrong and Susan P. Ashdown

Fabric for Fashion by Clive Hallett and Amanda Johnston

Fashion Illustration & Design by Manuela Brambatti

Fashionpedia by Fashionary

How To Start Sewing by Assembil Books

J. J. Pizzuto's Fabric Science Swatch Kit by Ingrid Johnson, Allen C. Cohen, and Ajoy K. Sarkar

New Complete Guide to Sewing by Reader's Digest

Pattern Magic by Tomoko Nakamichi

Patternmaking for Fashion Design by Helen Joseph-Armstrong

The Fashion Business Manual by Fashionary

The Sewing Book by Alison Smith

Websites

cfda.com

ecocult.com

fashionrevolution.org

goodonyou.eco

slowfactory.earth

thegoodtrade.com

Creators/Pages

Blueprint DIY

Brandi Joan

Cabrini Roy

Coolirpa

Daniela Tabois

Glory Allen

Kiana Bonollo

Kim Dave

Mimi G Style

Natalia Trevino Amaro

Nick Verreos

Paige Sechrist

Paola Gonzalez

The Essentials Club

The Modeliste Studio

The Sustainable Fashion Forum

Transformations by Tracy

With Wendy

Yolanda Espericueta

Zoe Hong

ACKNOWLEDGEMENTS

I didn't think I would be writing a book this early in my career, but the timing just made sense and aligned with where I am today. Before I pursued fashion design, I thought of becoming a fashion journalist. Ever since I was in elementary school, I have loved to write and enjoyed my English classes. I also had a blog in high school filled with my DIYs and OOTD, titled *Along the Lines of Ysabel*. This feels like such a surreal, full-circle moment that will quite literally be documented and remembered for decades to come.

First off, I'd like to thank the editor, Kelly Reed, and the entire Rocky Nook team who made this book happen for taking a chance on me. I have *never* written a book before, but to be given the opportunity to do so has been an incredible learning experience that I'll forever be grateful for. Kelly contacted me about two months after I graduated college. At the time, I was honestly still figuring out my next move. I remember she said, "I'm sorry if I'm giving you some homework," but this is the best "homework" assignment I've ever been given.

Thank you to my high school Creative Writing and English teacher, Ms. Weuve, for answering all of my questions before pursuing this opportunity. Your class made such a huge impact on me as a writer and a person, and I'm sure many of my classmates would also agree.

To my parents, Susie and Apollo, and my brother, Jordan, I can't thank you enough for all the sacrifices you've made during my fashion design journey since Day 1. My parents have never discouraged me from pursuing my dreams. I asked my dad to pull out my Lola's sewing machine from the shed when I was 13, and here I am today. Also, a huge thank you to my brother who let me turn his video-game room into my sewing and design studio.

ALL PHOTOS BY MIKAEL-ANGELO TE

Thank you to my Lola and Lolo for reminding me as I was growing up to excel in everything I do and that they'll support me along the way. I don't see them often because they are 6,000 miles away living their best life in Guam, but they have always been so prominent in my life. I cherish every moment with them.

Thank you to my Auntie Claire (Tita Neneng, to me) for being a large part of my sewing and fashion journey. My mom, Auntie Claire, and I would often go on shopping trips to the LA Fashion District ever since I was a kid. As a creative woman herself, she supported me in many ways, from taking me to a fashion design camp that I dreamt of attending and even buying us matching serger machines.

Thank you to my Auntie Louella for inspiring me to be a fashion icon. Growing up, I loved to see all the outfits she put together to match her eclectic, casual style. To this day, whenever she does a closet clean-out, I'm always the first to go through the bags. My goddaughter, Romi, is definitely going to be the next fashionista in the making!

Thank you to my boyfriend, Justin Castro, who is my righthand man in everything I do. You literally get the full experience. To name a few: You've walked around the fabric district with me during a heat wave. You've learned how to capture my favorite angles in content for social media. Not to mention, you've come as my plus one to all influencer events (we even went to NYC!), assisted me behind the scenes at every photo shoot and fashion show, and so much more. I'm blessed to make these memories with you by my side as we pursue what we love to do in the fashion industry.

To all my aunties, uncles, cousins, and relatives on both sides of my family (as a Filipino family, there's just way too many people to individually mention!), thank you for being in my life. Whether you've liked my parents' Facebook post of me modeling an outfit I made or attended one of my events, I am so grateful to be loved by you all.

To all my besties, (you know who you are), thank you for being supportive in everything that I do. Some of you I've known for over a decade and some just in the last few years, but you've all made an impact in my life. Now that I'm done with this book…let's go to Disneyland, Vegas, or Japan soon?

To my photographer and longtime friend, Ashley Chang, it's crazy to see how far we've come since meeting at Quest Dance Studio back in middle school. It is truly an honor to work with you. Thank you for being a part of this unique opportunity with me. Your passion for your craft is visible throughout all of these photographs, and you've executed this entire project beautifully.

Special thanks to Martin Mamangun for assisting Ashley and giving your all to this project. We are truly so thankful that you were able to be there and make the shoot run smoothly.

Thank you to Mikael-Angelo Te for helping capture these timeless, behind-the-scenes moments. I cherish the friendship we've formed over the last few years, and it's always a pleasure to work with you on all the different projects that we've presented to each other. Also, thank you to Janelle Angcaco and Grace Tran for coming along to help out and capture candid moments behind the scenes.

Thank you to Jaron Ramos for helping me style the entire shoot for this book. This was one of the few times I've worked so closely with a stylist on a project so special to me, and you understood my entire vision perfectly, even with the small amount of time.

To all of my beautiful models: Judimae Angcaco, Malia Azucenas, Raven Howard, and Leeza Vivas, thank you for bringing my clothes to life and giving your all to each look. I'm so appreciative to have worked with all of you on multiple projects over the years.

And to the entire community I've built through social media…THANK YOU, THANK YOU, THANK YOU. Without you, this would not have been possible, and I owe it to you all for this opportunity. From posting my DIYs and designs for ten people to see to now thousands of people worldwide, it's such an honor being able to share my journey with you all. I plan on doing this for the rest of my life. I hope to have inspired so many of you to pursue what you want to do in life. I promise you that if it's truly meant to be and you're passionate about making something happen, everything will fall into place.

I love and appreciate you so much!

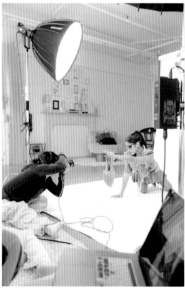

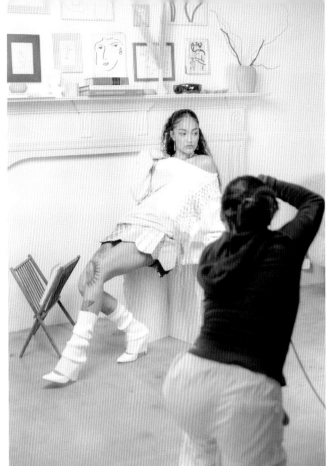

PHOTO BY MARTIN MAMANGUN